AF395166

DEAL HEAL GROW

DEAL HEAL GROW

30 Days To More Inner Peace

SHARI GREEN

www.sharigreencoaching.com

CONTENTS

This book is for you and all the women who have struggled to define their worlds past traumas. This book is for women that have a hard time finding their voices. I wrote this book for the daughters that watched stress materialize into illness in their mothers.

This book is a byproduct of my love for my family and God. Ahmaad, Nicholas, Grace, and Mateo, you each have shown me the importance of living and loving in the now. Thank you all for sharing your love with me unconditionally. To my heavenly father, God, you are my defender, way maker, and reason for being. I love you and am so gracious for your agape love towards me. I am who you say I am!

Have you ever felt like your emotions were overwhelming? So overwhelming that you considered quitting. You know you can't quit life, but you thought about it. Have you ever thought if only I were given different circumstances? Surely if I had an inheritance I wouldn't have to struggle so hard or would I?

Have you ever found yourself trying to pray away the pain, but it just keeps coming back? You think God, do you hear me? Have you ever thought, why do I keep going through the same challenges over and over again? If your answer is yes to any of these questions, please know you are not alone.

We seem to struggle with seeing ourselves how God sees us. We shy away from the discomfort of facing our true feelings and instead pour ourselves into more productivity. We find ways to get the job, start the business, and get our external needs met while struggling to find long-lasting fulfillment in any of them. What we are experiencing is just the result of our emotional needs not being met. How do you meet a need you don't know you have? How do you give yourself something you have never seen?

More and more women are searching for answers that will bring some ease to the emotional challenges we each face daily. Women are juggling households, businesses, and careers all while trying to manage their mental health. Not to mention that we are doing all of this while trying to unlearn and unpack layers of generational curses. We often find significance in how much we can take on and burn ourselves out before we can truly begin to create the impact we were designed for. I am here to tell you that just because you experience feelings of anxiety, depression, or insecurities at times doesn't mean there is something wrong with you or that you have a mental illness. It certifies that you are indeed a human being having a very real human experience. How well you navigate your experience is affected by your representation of yourself and the world around you. I am here to remind you that where you feel weak, God is your strength, and his love for you not only covers you but makes his wisdom available to you. Life brings some challenging experiences, and it is through the wrestling of our faith and challenging our beliefs that we learn to thrive in spite of any of them. Mental health has had this historic stigma that we are weak if we seek some mental support. That isn't true, and I will show you how to understand your mind so that you can heal and adopt new beliefs that will support the sound mind God has given you.

Do not let others define how your life should look; instead, start defining your life for yourself rooted in love and with an abundant mindset. You can use God's wisdom and your mind to heal beyond your pains, I will teach you how.

Feel free to write whatever thoughts and feelings come up for you in your book. This is your safe space.

CHAPTER 1

Rules Of Healing

1. My healing is a journey I get to take.

2. Healing is about me experiencing the love of God so deeply that it free's me from needing to repay my pain.

3. My healing shouldn't be judged.

4. I have the right to create boundaries as I heal.

5. I have permission to heal at my own pace.

6. To be healed and whole is why I was created.

7. It is okay to seek a new environment as I pursue my healing.

8. It is okay if other people don't understand the importance of my healing because I do.

9. As I become more aware, I won't judge others for not being as far along as me.

10. I must heal my internal world if I want to see healing in my external world.

11. I can create my own safe space to explore what has wounded me.

12. I may be wounded but, I am not broken. I don't require fixing, just nurturing.

CHAPTER 2

Your Basic Needs

What do you need right now? You may be thinking of a trip to Target, white sands in the Maldives, your favorite takeout, a Netflix binge, and a bank account that's endless. I'm not mad at any of these things, but let's be honest about where you really are. Your not truly happy, at least not most of the time. You have gotten so good at perfecting your "all is well" response for others that you haven't taken the time to ask yourself, "How am I really?" You spend your time thinking of more and more things to add to your life hoping once you finally have or do them, you will be set free from the stresses of life. You put off your healing because you don't know who you will become apart from the things you have learned to grudgingly accept. Believe me, I know because over the years I found myself there time and time again. I had gotten so good at looking like I was well in public while avoiding all my repressed anger and sadness that had already begun to alter my heart. I had become hardened towards people and discovering truth beyond my personal biases. I felt deep down that life wasn't fair and that somehow I was just given a bad hand. My pains started to grow stronger and were coming out as outbursts towards those I love and were called to serve. I wanted to escape my routine of self-pity, only fixing my symptoms, and just surviving my life. I was afraid that facing my pain meant discovering something I wouldn't have the strength to feel. I thought it would force me to lose more than I had already lost. One day I was crying on my bedroom floor, calling out to God and I heard a voice say, "Do you want to be healed?" This was a big moment for me because I had accepted my emotional avoidance to be a normal part of my life. I had succumbed to the programming of the world that says to suck it up and keep it moving. That one question taught me I was no longer a bystander in my life, I had a say so in how it could change moving forward. I began writing, researching, and crying till my eyes were red and puffy. My mind and body began detoxing all my unexpressed pain and it felt amazing. I started to realize what I was truly in need of and I started to see that I had a set of basic needs that I needed to learn how to meet from the inside out. These basic needs were what I had been trying to meet my entire life. You may think that you are driven by your desires, but you are truly driven by something far deeper within yourself. Every woman has the same basic needs. Her desires come from what she believes will fulfill those needs. There is a need for her identity, security, autonomy, growth, connection, and contribution. Every woman you know is striving to meet these needs and how it looks depends on how she views herself and the world around her.

How you **identify** yourself is not only essential for your well-being, it guides your convictions. Your convictions are the standards by which you live your life. Your identity tells you who you are and what you should expect of yourself because of who you are. When a woman lacks the conviction of her true identity she will look to others to define one for her and she will find herself bound to their fleeting opinions. If you identify as a woman with Christian values, then you will strive to live a life that brings glory to God. But what happens to the woman that has made people her God? She will tire herself out instead of leading her life from the space of grace that has been given to her by the one and only true God. What do you think happens when how you identify yourself is limited to your performance? You will constantly seek ways to place yourself in situations where you must perform in order to feel enough. So essentially your belief of who you are is directing how seen or unseen you become to yourself. It feels well to have others clap for us, but it nourishes our souls when we are able to clap for ourselves out of the integrity by which we live in alignment with who we are. If you see yourself as unworthy, you will produce behaviors that show that you are not yet sure of your value. If you see yourself as the "responsible one" of your family you may constantly feel like you have to do everything. "If I don't do it, it won't get done." Sounds familiar? Identity fulfills your need for significance.

It's the reason we have hashtags, movements, and social groups. It's the reason we seek status and degrees. The issue isn't holding a degree, title, or even being a part of a movement because God can use us in any space. The issue comes when we limit our significance to whether or not we have those things. Having a way to identify ourselves brings us a sense of belonging. It gives us permission to be who we are without judgment. What happens when you identify yourself by your shortcomings and not as the image barrier of Christ you truly are? You will find yourself limiting your potential and self-sabotaging every opportunity you get to do what you were called to do in your life. How you choose to identify yourself, comes from what you were exposed to as a child. Think of the ways you saw your parents or care takers identifying themselves. Have you chosen to identify the same way or did you choose the complete opposite? Scientists say that by the age of 5 we each have developed our view of ourselves and the way we see the world based on the environment we grew up in. Imagine that, by the age of 5 you already had a biased lens through which you saw your whole world. Do you see any proof of that in your life now?

If you grew up in a religious environment that lacked integrity you probably at some point rebelled against it. It becomes hard to follow God when the representatives in your life of God aren't showing the true love of God towards you or you fail to see any fruit of his teachings in their lives. That is how I felt. It took for me to have a personal experience that showed me who God really was and why I needed him in my life. If you didn't receive much validation, attention, or security growing up you may find yourself wanting to be more independent. It's that need for significance. Your independence also gives you a sense of certainty. You may think to yourself that if I can fulfill my own desires then I won't have to experience the disappointment of others failing to meet my desires. You may think that if you can create more control of your world then you can lessen your chances of experiencing pain. What does pain represent for you? Why have you spent so much time unwilling to take risks in your life out of fear of possible pain? There are pains that are inflicted on us by people and some that just come by way of living, but both can serve our good. We don't get to experience the revelation of our pains until we become willing to acknowledge them. You are living to meet your needs based on your biased views and those views get a lot clearer once you have given yourself a chance to process your pain. If not, you can end up doing the right things for the wrong reasons or doing the wrong things for the right reasons. I want to help you discover what is true for you so that you can pursue the right things for the right reasons in your life.

If you struggle to feel significant you may think if I can become XYZ, then others will see that I am valuable. You begin striving and hoping that if others feel you are valuable then so will you but no amount of admiration from other people will be able to change the beliefs you hold about yourself only you can do that. You must decide to believe that you are valuable and start looking for the evidence in your life. If you struggle with neglecting your own needs it may be from not having your needs met as a child, so in order to adapt you focus on the needs of others hoping to keep them around. Having people around makes you feel safe. Your need for **security** is why you fear losing people from your life. This fear can cause you to keep people in your life that continue to cause you more harm than good. Let's pause for a second.

Take a look in the mirror. Who do you see? I wonder if you truly see yourself? Do you see how your smile lights up a room? Do you see how confident you are when you are living out your passions? Do you see your soul glow when you are treated well? Or how your encouraging words push others to keep on fighting? Or the way your husband's heartthrobs when he sees you happy? Do you know how your presence makes those around you feel seen? Or the way your child sees you as an unconditional shield of protection? What about the way your coworkers admire your leadership? You only see yourself in parts, there is much more to who you are. Oftentimes people get the best parts of you, but what if you got to experience the best parts of you too? You have to grow to see your worth. No one knows all that you overcome daily or all that you have been through, but you do. And because you do, you should be proud of yourself. Your need for admiration is not a negative thing, it's a part of your humanity. I do believe that God intended for your identity and security to come from him, that way it could never be taken away by anyone.

Can I tell you a secret? Everyone struggles with their identity at some point in their life. Even when you discover it, you have to remind yourself constantly that what you know about yourself is true. We call these struggles insecurities. In a world where comparison is encouraged, it can become easy to feel insecure or unsure of who you truly believe you are. We can thank God for his grounded wisdom though. He took away all the guesswork and created us all in his image. Imagine in our various unique shades, features, and personalities we each are a reflection of him. So if you want to know more of who you are, get to know more of who God is.

You see no one can give you the significance you are seeking, it is in your DNA. You can try to find your significance in being a mother or being a wife, but even those roles will fall short to meet your needs at times. Think of the wife that becomes a widow, is she no longer significant? Think of the woman who can't seem to find the spouse of her dreams, is she no longer significant? What about the woman that struggles with infertility, is she no longer significant? Your significance comes from God, the one who knows your beginning and your end. The one that has created you to impact this world through your testimonies and gifts. The one that truly knows the limitless potential that lies within you. When do you feel the most significant? Is it when other's are praising you? Is it when you feel needed? Is it when you are making your own money? Growing your personal awareness of what makes you feel important can help you to discover how you currently get your needs met. Once you discover any of your needs that are being met in an unhealthy way, you can decide to change them.

In my twenties, I found my identity in my career. I'd come from a family that focused on education and making sure you get a job to pay bills and have something to show for yourself. I struggled with this train of thought because deep inside myself a voice was telling me to dream bigger. Education and finding a career are both blessings and are helpful when attached to your life's assignment. Knowledge without vision creates ego, not impact. What I wasn't told growing up was that God had already designed a purpose for my life. I thought picking an esteemed profession was my purpose. We use the word purpose so much, but what is it truly? Your purpose is the assignment God created for your life. That life might not look how everyone thinks it should look, and that is okay. I constantly desired more than working to pay bills, but I wanted my family's admiration more than following my path fully. I identified myself with the beliefs that I learned from them. So when my life didn't look like those beliefs, I questioned my significance. I wanted to feel like I was enough, and I didn't know at the time that I could be enough without everyone's approval. We learn as children how to establish rapport with those we admire and love with hopes they will love us back.

Establishing rapport can be an excellent tool for building fulfilling relationships with others, but it works best when used out of a space of abundance, not insecurity. You want to build connections with people from a space of love, not obligation. We can find ourselves trying to act more like others in hopes that we will find acceptance. Is acceptance indeed acceptance if you aren't truly yourself? I would notice that I received more praise if I worked for a well-known company or got some fancy title. I have had so many jobs, and it's not because I am a Jamaican. It's because I was constantly seeking to feel significant. All that time, I knew I wanted to be an entrepreneur, but I didn't know many women in my family that had become one, let alone any who would encourage me to be one. Every family has its trouble makers. You know the ones that question all the traditions and do things that look crazy to everyone else. It only looks crazy until it works.

It was my desire for identity and connection that had me for years straddling the fence and delaying committing fully to what I felt my purpose was. Think about it. Isn't it crazy to think that we could make significant life decisions to feel accepted, but women do it every day? If you are not careful you will hold yourself as a prisoner to the thoughts of others who themselves aren't even happy in their own lives. As I have matured, I have also become more confident in owning my choices and my life.

Most women want to assume full responsibility for their lives but they are afraid of the accountability that comes with it. Failure is often frowned upon so they think they have to be perfect. No one is perfect and trying to be perfect isn't relatable. Perfection doesn't impact lives, authenticity does.

Today I focus on how I want to feel each day and who I want to become. You don't have to race when you're pursuing your purpose, you will be guided by your own timeline. Just live! I have also learned that my family loved me no matter what I did. It was me that didn't understand that I didn't need their approval to have their love. We grow up in families that don't always know how to show love in a way that feels good to us. Society has functioned this way for generations. This mindset that thinks everyone should think, be, and believe as I do or else is killing many relationships all over the world. Families should be able to enjoy and support each other without needing to judge and project personal views onto each other. Let God be the judge.

We are not just driven by significance but by our need for security. That is why you feel fearful. It's the idea that you won't be able to manage or survive the pain. Menstrual cramps and childbirth has proven otherwise. Even the most painful of feelings eventually subside. God warns us that in this life, we will have pain. The pain we experience will build us up in endurance. Think to all the moments you thought you wouldn't get past something, but you did. You became more assertive, wiser, and better for it. Pains are necessary for our growth.

Do you find yourself often trying to control everything? You are seeking a level of predictability. Taking control of things gives you a sense of security. When you are not secure in your identity, you will often struggle to have faith and feel a need to control the world around you. Managing your decisions and goals is excellent; trying to dictate the choices and responses of others not so much. It's your responsibility to dictate your response, not the response of others. What would your life look like if you become okay with being yourself while accepting the differences of others?

Speaking of control, have you ever felt the frustration of someone attempting to control you? That frustration comes from your need for **autonomy**. Autonomy is your desire to make your own choices. I grew up with very little autonomy, so to meet that need, I became very rebellious. I thought I needed to be more aggressive in my tone to get what I needed because that is what I saw. I also saw that you could manipulate people into doing what you wanted them to do. We were being programmed by the behaviors in our environments and we have to become brave enough to change the ones that are unhealthy. I rebelled constantly to feel some sense of having my own way. I would purposefully go against the decisions others would try to make for me. When we attempt to control every aspect of how someone else should experience the world, we rob them of autonomy. We each meet the need for autonomy in a variety of ways. My rebellious nature taught me that I was often only hurting myself and putting my relationships in jeopardy. I had the belief that the only way to have some say so in my life was to go against others. I have learned a different way of expressing my need to have input in the choices that affect me. I can now set clear boundaries when I feel someone is overstepping how involved they feel they should be in my decision-making. I communicate by saying things like, " that doesn't make me feel well, that doesn't work for me, not right now, or let me give it some thought." The goal is to give yourself a moment to process the information coming at you so that you can respond thoughtfully, even in stressful situations. Don't ever feel rushed to respond to everything right away; consider the level of urgency. You have to let people know what works for you.

Do you know what would happen if everything in your life was sure? You would be bored out of your mind, that's what. You need **growth**. Life creates endless opportunities for you to grow. Some of those opportunities involve instant gratification, while others involve an ongoing challenge. You probably call those challenges problems. Isn't it funny how when we get a raise, a free meal, or a new opportunity, we are ecstatic for the increase, but when the increase involves us stepping outside of our everyday comfort, we find it hard to invite it into our lives? It all comes down to the beliefs you choose to hold, and by the end of this book, I will teach you how to challenge your thoughts to have ones that support you being your highest self.

The fifth need that you have is the need for **connection**. You are a spiritual being having a human experience. You exist to have a relationship with God and fellowship with other people. Connection cultivates love. You are made from and with love. Love can build you up and leave you feeling so fulfilled. It starts with you receiving God, unconditionally. You do not need to change any part of yourself before God can be present with you. Start tracing his love in your life. Think of the unexplainable moments that you were kept safe, made it through pain, found the strength to move forward. When is the last time you wrote down all the ways you have seen God show up for you? That love lives within you. You will not always feel filled with love, especially when you need recharging. But that doesn't change the fact that it is true. Love isn't just a feeling; it's a commitment to your well-being. God is committed to securing your well-being.

Do you genuinely know love, or has love for you been wrapped up in conditions? Most women settle for connection because true love seems too scary. So you connect physically and mentally, never truly investing your most vulnerable emotions with others. That is why couples can be married for over 20 years and still not feel truly seen by each other. They are still trying to hide the fragile parts of themselves. They have not learned yet, how the other person feels most loved. Instead, they love each other through their strategy for receiving love. You can be in a relationship where you bare all physically, but not emotionally. You may fear that the person will judge you or reject you because growing up that is what you experienced. Unresolved pain creates walls in your heart. I will show you how to tear them down so that you can experience authentic connection and love in all of your relationships. How would your life be if you had more genuine connections and love in your life? How would your life be better if you knew you could be yourself without changing the people around you?

When we feel like we are enough, we can see the true value in others. We also become more accepting of others in our lives and learn to serve them without expectations. **Contribution** is your sixth basic need. Making someone else's day better is one of the best natural pain reliever's. When you see the positive impact you can have on people; it gives your life so much more meaning. Your need for contribution explains why you are so solution-driven. You may not see yourself as a leader, but you are. Leaders see solutions to problems and live by their desire to make things better. Have you ever wondered why when you see others hurting, you feel a strong impulse to help? Your leadership skills show up without you even noticing. You have many gifts that can serve you and so many others. Have you ever heard the saying healed people heal people? As we begin healing ourselves, we find it easier to give more significant levels of contribution. That contribution should come from our hearts, not our minds. We help others when we give them what they need and not what we think they need. The more aware you become of your needs, the more you will feel empowered to meet the needs of others in a way that feels good to them.

Circle the words that describe you

Outgoing Joyful Strong Creative Lovable
Resourceful Compassionate Kind Funny
Honest Beautiful Blessed
Peaceful Patient Trustworthy
Virtuous Outgoing Gracious

(Finish the sentence below)
Who am I? **I am a woman who is**

What do I currently do in my life to meet my need for identity, security, autonomy, growth, connection, and contribution?

CHAPTER 3

Your Childhood

We each have a story that we tell ourselves. It becomes this visual movie in our heads or maybe a still picture of how it happened or at least how we remember it happening. Memories can be a tricky thing. We only have our feelings to go off of after a moment has passed. Your memory is not the physical real moment, it is the representation of that experience that you have created. That is why two people can experience the same event, but there can be two different interpretations of what took place. Believe it or not, you are telling yourself a story each and every day of how life works for you. You know the story of what happened to you that made you the way you are. It's the same story you use to justify your thoughts, beliefs, and behaviors. The pain you felt from your childhood is very real, but the meaning you hold around your experiences may not be the full truth. You can assume those that hurt you meant it, but do you truly know that to be true? People operate at their level of awareness and how they believe they will get their needs met. When an adult is struggling with their own unresolved trauma and negative behaviors they often reintroduce the same or similar traumas onto their children most times unknowingly. When the stories we carry in our minds aren't based on the total truth we can find ourselves creating our lives through a false filter in hopes of avoiding our childhood pains all over again. You begin to self-sabotage love and success in your life. Self-sabotage is when your behaviors or thoughts don't match the life you truly desire to live because of underlying false beliefs you hold. Where do these behaviors and thoughts come from? Did you create them or did the environment you grew up in influence them?

For years I traveled with a story that placed me at the scene of a crime. I was the main victim in this story and the more I told it to myself, the more limitations I experienced in my life. It went like this... Imagine a sweet little girl filled with a sense of adventure and curiosity. Well, that sweet little girl was me and all she ever wanted was to feel accepted. I remember one day I was about 5 years old, standing in the walkway of our apartment. We had just moved to Georgia from New York City. At the time my mom was the only one working outside the home, while my dad stayed home with me. I remember going to daycare in the mornings. Every afternoon the daycare van would drop me off at home and my dad would take me inside and make me spaghetti. I use to love spaghetti, it was all my dad would or maybe could make and it made me feel so cared for. I don't remember how it tasted but my dad made it for me, that was all that mattered. I can still remember hearing lamb chops play along television show playing on my small box television set. To this day a good meal and my favorite show is still one of my favorite past times. I had really sweet memories of my dad, until one day it all changed for me. One day my mom had returned home from work and what I heard next truly affected me. I can still remember the look on her face. The look on my mom's face was different from the bright smile I was used to. She looked tired and sad. We only had one car at the time and I remember feeling what I know now as feelings of anxiety. See when our minds don't have a mental representation of something that is happening, we feel confused, rejected, or afraid. I had never seen my parents have an interaction like that before, so I didn't know how to interpret it.

My mom was having a heated conversation with my dad about him using the car. I can't tell you exactly all that was said, but I will never forget the scary look on my father's face. I remember him yelling at her and saying words that made me feel so afraid. At that moment my mind developed a very strong belief. The belief that men were not a safe space and that my dad didn't love me or my mom. Now was that true? No, It wasn't but that was my interpretation. You see as children we may not understand the fullness of our experiences, but we remember the energy we felt. Our minds take inventory of our experiences, it then begins to delete, distort, and generalize pieces of those experiences to ultimately give us labels for our safety. I had cast my dad as an angry man and if I am honest most of my memories of him growing up involve him yelling, looking at me with displeasure, or being passive-aggressive. What we don't understand as children is that people are not their behaviors. My dad wasn't an angry man, he was an unhappy one. There were things that he did that hurt my feelings deeply, but I don't believe today that those were his intentions. In fact, the father I know today is very loving, funny, and supportive of me.

It took many years, growing in my self-awareness, and several therapists for me to be able to gain that perspective. When those responsible for your emotional support fail to address how their emotions and behaviors have affected you, your self-worth withers. When the people you look to for safety and nurturing don't seem to acknowledge your pain you start to question if maybe you are the problem. When major life changes occur without your input and no one takes the time to help you process your emotions around them it can cause you to produce a variety of unhealthy behaviors that you only use because you feel they will keep you safe. You may think trauma is limited to extreme circumstances, but trauma is an emotional response to any terrible event in your life. Childhood traumas include but aren't limited to abandonment, divorce, sexual or physical abuse, car crashes, witnessing death, emotional neglect, and violence in the home. When you don't take the time to feel and work through the emotions that come as a result of trauma, those emotions grow stronger and manifest themselves in every area of your life. Women are not trash cans. We are not designed to store things in our bodies or minds that don't serve us being the best version of ourselves. The more we try to hide or suppress the mess within ourselves, the more external conflict we will essentially experience in our life. The emotions can not stay within you they will eventually come out as breakdowns, outbursts, attitudes, being critical of others, self-sabotaging behaviors, addictions, and so much more. These are all examples of the mind's solution to the pain you are experiencing based on the examples you have seen of how you should deal with pain. Those behaviors are your mind's way of saying you are overloaded with feelings that need to be dealt with. Your mind just wants the pain to subside. You can train your mind to adopt new healthy ways of navigating that pain that doesn't involve you inflicting more pain on yourself or others.

When I go back objectively in my memories of my father, I see a man in need of significance. I see a man that was truly uncertain and afraid. I believe he was trying to meet his own basic needs, not knowing how his way of doing so affected me or my mom. Growing up, whenever I would hear that familiar tone come from his mouth, those same feelings I felt that day when I was 5 would resurface. I am sure there were moments that I shared with him that could have been loving and safe, but my belief system wouldn't even allow for me to recognize them when they were happening. Not to mention that I don't know the full story of my parent's relationship. I will never understand the details and dynamics that played a part in my experience with them both. It took for me to see forgiveness as a necessity not just something nice to do to grow in forgiveness towards them both. Believe it or not, I learned that I had held resentment towards my mom as well. I blamed her for marrying an angry man. I felt that she should have protected me more. The emotional toxicity that is cultivated when we refuse to allow ourselves to forgive those who have hurt us, becomes our poison. What I realized is that everyone is operating at their level of consciousness, so the things that we each do that hurt others are due to the ignorance of our awareness. When we know better, we can do better. I am better today because of the lessons my traumas have taught me.

The mind is like a supercomputer that stores only the most crucial information. Some events that we experience can be so traumatic that our minds will decide it's better to delete its memory altogether. Our memories are like google searches that bring up quick labels to help us make quick decisions for our safety. See when your young, you are working with a limited frame of reference. What do I mean? You haven't had enough life experience or developed enough language to properly articulate nor process what everything means. Your unconscious mind stores your memories and creates labels for how you see the world, but what happens when your world changes? What happens when you become an adult but your emotional maturity still aligns with the kid version of yourself? Your beliefs have to evolve in order for your world to evolve. If a woman holds the label that most men are angry and selfish, what do you think she will find? Her thoughts and behaviors will unconsciously reflect that belief and her interactions with men will cause that belief to seem true. That is why it is so important that we begin uncovering our unconscious beliefs so that our behaviors won't lead us somewhere we don't truly want to go.

What is your earliest memory of your childhood? Does it bring you joy or does it bring you a level of pain? If you find yourself trying to avoid thinking of moments from your past, then there is some healing to do. How will I know that I am healed? You will know once the memory no longer holds the same emotions for you and you have found the value in the experience. Once you have accepted that people are not their behaviors, but are ignorant of the true pain their actions have caused others. Healing doesn't involve belittling how an experience has affected you. Healing is allowing your story to evolve in its meaning. Your life isn't ruined and your past doesn't have to dictate your future. Taking the time to see a professional therapist or counselor can create a safe space for you to unravel and learn how to rebuild your emotional health.

When we fail to care for our own needs, we fail to genuinely care for the needs of others that may look different than ours. Have you ever said to someone, "It's just not that serious!" Really? How do you know it's not serious to someone else? How do you know that what is happening, isn't affecting them deeply? Your need to protect the biases you have created in your own mind can cause you to be insensitive towards the biases that others hold in their own minds.

The most influential women of our time have learned to welcome the good and bad of their experiences, not letting the bad ones keep them from creating good ones for the future. They have learned to manage their belief systems and only keep the ones that serve who they want to become. It is up to you to decide which beliefs you will choose to hold or allow to define you going forward. It is up to you to become your first safe space by not judging your feelings.

In my coaching practice, I use several NLP (Neuro-Linguistic Programming) techniques. In short, NLP detects and modifies unconscious biases or limitations of a person's map of the world. And it does this through the conscious use of language. I became a certified NLP Practitioner after learning through therapy, that a lot of my present issues were coming from beliefs I developed in my childhood. You see therapy deals more with your past trauma, which prepares you for coaching. I was determined to learn a new way of seeing my world and now I get to help so many other women like you, find that same freedom. One of the activities I do with my clients is I help them to go back in time to any memory where they felt their basic needs weren't met. In the activity, we begin to identify what the need was. I walk them through accessing the current resources that they now hold. Resources can be love, compassion, patience, and so much more. Then we walk through them imagining themselves giving themselves exactly what they needed at that moment. It is a simple activity, but so powerful in how it transforms the feelings surrounding the memory. Remember you can change the beliefs you choose to hold, while still acknowledging the experience.

One of the most commonly used sayings in NLP is "the map is not the territory. This means that what you see or feel isn't all that you are experiencing. What you see is your world view, not necessarily the true view of the world. You may feel mad at what someone said to you, but it's not just what they said that made you mad. It's the belief around how what they said will affect you, that has you mad. Whatever it was feels to you like a threat to one of your basic needs. This all happens on the unconscious level, so there are times you will just react without being aware of the layers of beliefs that caused your reaction. The goal is to train your mind to access the right beliefs that will produce the behaviors you desire to have in your life. Sometimes, your inner child just needs to hear you say, that it is okay to move forward and forgive. Give yourself the gift of new understanding and true inner peace.

When you think of your childhood what words come to mind?

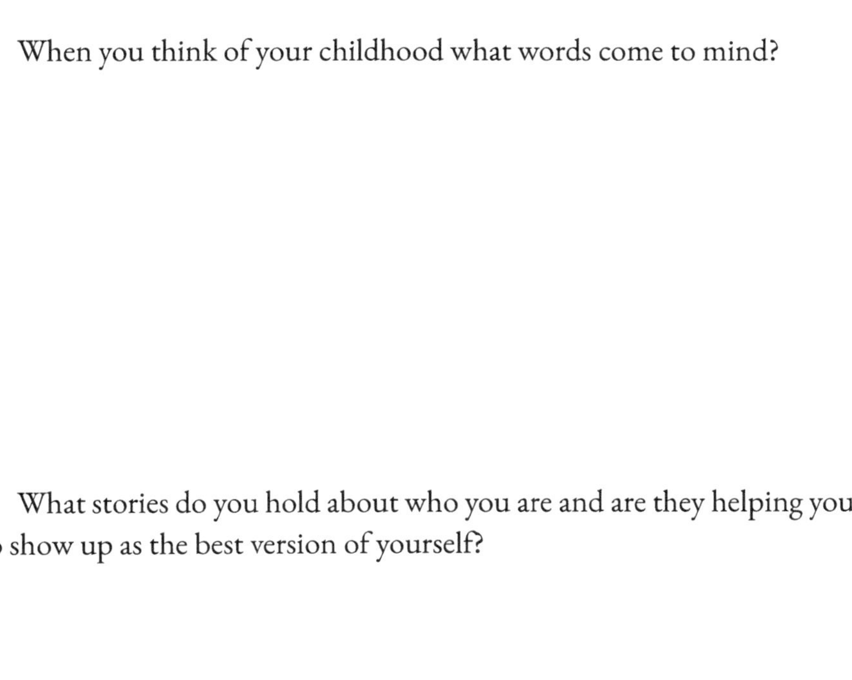

What stories do you hold about who you are and are they helping you to show up as the best version of yourself?

Does your story have to stay the same or can it evolve in its meaning? What meaning does your story hold for you?

What have you been able to accomplish, overcome, or help others with because of your experiences growing up?

CHAPTER 4

Your Beliefs

What do you believe about yourself? Better yet what have you been taught to believe about yourself and the world around you? I was talking to a friend one day and I asked her if she thought peace was something she should have to earn? She shared that after a hard day of work she looks forward to a peaceful evening. It made me think. Why don't we see peace as a daily necessity? Why is it that we expect our days to be filled with stress and busyness? Why don't we see peace as something we should have access to all day. Peace isn't something we earn it is something God offers us. Peace is a mindset. Peace is what God left us through Jesus. The peace of knowing everything in this world has already been conquered, even the things that cause you pain. What if you allowed peace to lead you into everything, instead of looking to everything to find peace?

I remember hearing growing up that black and minority women had to work 10 times harder than everyone else to be successful. Do you know what that created in me? A belief that I needed to be doing a million and one things all the time in order to be successful. I thought that if my life didn't match everyone else's then that would mean I wasn't doing enough. Have you ever felt that way? This belief has led me to burn out so many times, which has affected my mental and physical health. If your too busy, then your not present. Being present means not drifting backward to your past or far ahead to your future, but instead finding what you need most in your now. If you're not present with yourself, then your probably not present with others. You will find yourself just doing, but not intentionally being who you truly desire to be. I started challenging whether believing that I need to work harder than other ethnicities served me. More importantly, I asked myself, "Who do I show up as when I believe that to be true?"

We live in a world where that belief has been true and can still be seen as truth, however that is not the entire picture. We also live in a time where black women and minorities are doing things our ancestors could only dream of. We are our ancestor's dreams coming true. The walls that have been built to suppress our growth can't match us because we were designed to walk through them. That belief is true and feels more empowering to me. The goal is to see life as it truly is, but not worst than it truly is. This is what I have come to believe and have seen be true in my life, when I lean into what God has inspired me to do, it thrives. When I stay focused on my vision, goals, decisions, and my own development I thrive. Do you realize who you belong to? Do you not think that God's plans for your life are far greater than any systematic oppression? Do you realize that your obedience to God's will for your life might be the very solution to that system that has oppressed so many?

If you have managed to break the cycle of always needing to feel busy, you should be proud of yourself. If you aren't there yet, you can get there too. Start by getting clear on why you're doing what you are doing? Then ask yourself if it is truly helping you or others? Is it helpful to yourself or anyone if you are operating as a fraction of yourself? Get clear on your vision for your life and let that lead you through your days. You will find that some of the things you spend your time doing are only distractions from where your attention is truly needed.

Then there is the money conversation, most of us heard growing up. "That cost too much, money doesn't grow on trees?" Have you ever noticed how that has affected how you interact with money? When you believe money is scarce, your actions will produce evidence to support your belief. This is why you may find yourself often overspending until you find yourself in a space where money is scarce. Or you may believe that money is scarce and so you try everything in your power to hold on to it. Or you work yourself crazy with no clear plan of what you're going to do with the money and you spend it all until the money is scarce again. This belief may cause you to feel afraid to invest it in your personal development or to serve other people. Your afraid that all you have now is all you will ever have and that is just not true. Money is a tool. It is meant to circulate and to be used to create opportunity. Do you know what money is attracted to? Value. So if you want to attract more money into your life start creating more value for others. We live in the information age where you can learn also how to manage and invest. Think about, it does money make you happy? That rectangle sheet of paper itself doesn't make you happy. It's the things that money can afford you that make you happy. Like more time with those you love and more opportunities to help others in need.

If I was to ask you, do you want to be a millionaire, what would your response be? Does that thought make you feel uncomfortable? Or maybe your thinking yes, bring on the millions! The point I am trying to make here is not that you should or should not desire to be a millionaire. The point is that you shouldn't limit what is possible for you, your family, or those you can help by having a false belief around money's purpose in your life. No matter your desire the goal is to know that whatever you need is available to you. "When the student is ready, the teacher will appear" (Buddha Siddhartha). When you show that you can manage money, more money will be available to you. Stop telling yourself all the reasons why it can't happen for you and start asking how it can? The is no lack concerning you, you are God's daughter. The only lack you may experience is a lack of perspective. If you are unwilling to shift and become the kind of person that can create more value, then be honest with yourself about it. Maybe you're afraid and uncertain. As long as you realize that your issue was never that money was scarce, your issue was the mindset that you held about what was available to you. You may not have had money, but you have creativity and that alone is enough. The idea that suggests that only a certain race or gender can have access to luxury and resources has to end. We live in an era where resources find those that seek them and luxury can belong to anyone that desires it. You have to learn to be objective in your beliefs, or else your beliefs may hold you back from creating new experiences.

Let's talk a bit more about how our beliefs are formed. When I was a young girl I was very curious about everything. I loved talking and since I didn't get to talk much at home, boy did I talk at school. I remember it was time for report cards to come out. I had good grades, but in the comment section the teacher wrote, "Shari talks too much." When I got home I remember my dad scolding me for talking at school. It wasn't just what he said, it was the disappointment I felt from him. That was painful for me as a child. I started to believe that if I talked too much then people would be disappointed in me. I believed that no matter what I did if I wasn't how they thought I should be, then I wasn't good enough. What do you think happened next? I grew up watching everything I said and became super critical of myself and others. I also started striving to be perfect. Can you imagine my frustration with myself after realizing over and over that perfection couldn't be obtained? I took those beliefs into my adulthood and it turned into people-pleasing. I would say yes to things that I truly wanted to say no to. I would sit in work meetings, fake laughing at things I didn't find funny just to fit in. Why do we do this to ourselves? It all comes back to those underlying beliefs we hold. We have two main categories in our minds that hold beliefs. One is labeled pain and the other is labeled pleasure. Our minds sort our experiences and let us know which ones bring pain and which ones bring pleasure. This can be extremely helpful as we think, choose, and feel our way through life, but it can be hurtful when we tell ourselves that certain things bring us pleasure that is truly harmful to us.

Beliefs can run so deep to the point where questioning them will scare you. The more time we spend thinking something is true, the more our brains become wired to carry our beliefs. It can bring up fear because if you choose to adopt a new belief then it can threaten your certainty. Remember that basic need we all have. Change is scary. Change involves challenging the status quo and the reality of that may feel unfamiliar to you. A new belief may even mean you having to take some responsibility for your behaviors. Most people have a hard time taking responsibility for their behaviors, in fact, they often blame someone else or even God for why something happened. Taking responsibility for your actions can be tough when you already struggle to feel like your enough, but taking responsibility can help you to take on new positive actions for your future.

You have to start rewiring what you tell yourself is pleasure and what you tell yourself is pain.

Have you ever dated someone that was bad for you? I mean he left you drained and frustrated almost every day. You knew in your heart that you should leave the relationship but you were so scared to pull the plug. What do you think took you so long to walk away? Was it the fear of being alone? What was it about being alone that seemed so scary? We're you alone as a child once and it left you feeling afraid? You don't know how to process being alone as a child because you don't know what to expect. When your young you need direction because your life experience is limited by your lack of experience. Now that you are an adult, you now know that being physically by yourself doesn't have to feel scary. You see if you are still traveling your adult life with childhood fears, then you will limit yourself by thinking life can only look one way. Have you seen that being alone is not so bad, in fact, it becomes amazing when you are in need of some me-time? It all goes back to what you believe will meet your needs. What if you started to create beliefs that support your needs but also don't compromise the life you truly want? What if you set healthy boundaries in your life? What would that feel like in your life?

Boundaries are expectations that you create and express that support your values for your life. They help you to only say yes when you mean it and to say no even when you're scared to say it. Your boundaries may change as your beliefs change. Life has a way of always challenging what we believe. Something happens to us and we have to question all that we thought was true. Have you ever heard the saying, "people come into your life for a reason, season, or a lifetime?" I believe everything that comes into your life is happening for you to grow.

I dated this guy once that changed how I saw myself in such an impactful way. I was hanging out at his house one day and I started to get hungry. I wasn't familiar with the area he lived in so I asked him for some suggestions. There was a Chick-fil-A and a Subway nearby but I decided I really wanted Chick-fil-A. He was working at the time, so I decided to run by myself to go grab the food. After about 10 minutes of the GPS leading me in the wrong direction, I decided to go to the Subway instead. I didn't really want Subway, but I was so frustrated from driving all around. I got back to his house and he said, " I'm so glad you got your food. Wait!" He noticed that I had a Subway bag in my hand. He asked me why I had Subway? I told him that I couldn't find Chick-fil-A and just settled on Subway. He asked me why I didn't call him? I told him that I didn't want to bother him. What he said next, I had never been asked before. He said, "Shari! Why would you settle for something you didn't want when you were able to get what you truly wanted?" I thought about it and honestly, I didn't know why. I had spent so much of my life settling for things I didn't truly want and I guess I had come to believe that it was okay. We talked about it and I finally understood that what he wanted me to understand was bigger than my lunch. He wanted me to see myself as deserving of what I knew was best for me. I will always be grateful for that lesson because it has changed so much of how I see myself and the world today.

Have you ever found yourself in a position where you settled for less than you truly desired? Why did you? What did you believe about yourself that held you back? You have an opportunity now to never settle again. Some people believe that God causes us to settle. I just don't believe that to be true. God's plans for us may look different than we expect but his plans will never cause us to settle because he is intentional. In fact, God says to seek him for understanding before you do anything. How often do you do that? That way you can move in alignment with his purpose for your life. Thankfully he gives us grace for our mistakes and disobedience, so even when we find ourselves out of alignment he loves us back to where we need to be.

I want you to take inventory of your life. In the areas where you feel the least fulfilled, notice what beliefs you hold in those areas? Do you notice any that are causing you that lack of fulfillment? What are you going to do about them? I know it can seem scary to make changes in your life, but your current preferences are not life or death. Your whole world is not going to fall apart because you decided to make changes for the better. Instead of being afraid of what could happen, have faith in all that will happen once you decide to release all that no longer serves you.

"Walk by faith, not by sight." (2 Corinthians 5:7) I interpret this scripture as God saying Live by faith, not by sight. If you live by what you see you will always feel restricted by the present moment. If you choose to live by faith you will feel the sweet embrace of the unlimited potential that life has to offer you. It is okay to change how you once saw something to be true, you were created to evolve.

What beliefs can you start holding about yourself that will support you feeling successful, loved, at peace, and more confident about your life?

EX: I want things to be okay and they eventually will be. I have the tools and resources to handle and get through them. I have been able to overcome hard things, I can do it again.

CHAPTER 5

Your Behaviors

Believe it or not, people are not their behaviors. This can be hard to accept when you have experienced painful interactions with people in your life. It can be even harder to accept if you grew up being labeled by your behaviors. Behaviors are a function of our state of mind. You have an experience, which produces a feeling, and that feeling produces a behavior. Where do we learn these behaviors? In our childhoods and throughout our lives. We mirror behaviors that we see from our parents, television, and all around us. Have you ever felt stressed or upset and someone asked you "Are you okay?" You then reply with "I'll be okay." Why do you think you do this? It's because you have seen people in your life do this. That is why suppressing your emotions feels like normal behavior for you because you grew up around other people that did the same. Somewhere in your observation of life growing up, you got the message that it is okay to tend to your feelings later. We often normalize behaviors that truly don't feel well to our souls and it's time to uncover why.

Think of a toddler who hasn't yet learned to talk. They will throw tantrums and throw objects to get their needs met. They don't know yet how to tell you what they want, so they try other forms of communication to let you know. When you constantly get your way by throwing tantrums and you never develop the language to articulate your needs, guess what happens? You grow into an adult that still has outbursts you just no longer roll around on the floor. Did you know communication is not just verbal? You are constantly communicating with your body, vocal tone, touch, and even your eyes.

As parents, we are all guilty of compromising in our responses towards our children at times because we want peace and we want it now. We may find ourselves under stressful conditions giving in to the tantrums of not just our children but even other adults. What we have to keep in mind for our children is that one day they will become adults and the standards that we set for them now will be the standards they will follow until they learn something different. When it comes to addressing tantrums in adults you always want to address the behavior, not the adult in the calmest way possible. You can use that moment to show them what will get your attention instead of how they are currently behaving. We teach people how to interact with us by what we chose to react to.

Have you ever been told by someone that you have an attitude? And you reply, "I don't have an attitude." The person has noticed some level of change in your tone, posture, or even hand gestures that suggest you are not happy with them. We can be in a bad state of mind and not even be conscious of it. So when someone points out to you that you have an attitude, instead of increasing in frustration, you should ask them what you are doing that makes them think you have an attitude? You should ask yourself if there is anything making you upset at that moment? We often try to hide how we are truly feeling and sometimes those feelings will start spilling out and we won't even notice them. Acknowledging how we feel more often can help us to become more aware and create new healthy behaviors in our lives.

Do you know someone that always gossips about people? I mean they are always looking for a flaw in someone else. Have you ever thought about what state of mind they may be speaking out of? Have you ever in your life gossiped about someone? Tell the truth. That isn't who you are though, is it? No, it's not. We are much more than our behaviors, but our behaviors betray us when we choose them with the wrong state of mind. Your state of mind comes from what you focus on. That is why God tells us to renew our minds daily because we live in a world full of distractions and every distraction is not good for our state of mind.

I worked at my son's school for one year. I am so thankful for that time. I use to peek in on him while he was learning, hug him tight in the hallway, and be there to have his back when someone wasn't meeting his needs. I have what I call a "grace-based" relationship with my Nicholas. It's a relationship that is based on the mutual understanding that we both are imperfect, yet constantly growing into who God says we are. We have an ongoing working relationship rooted in mutual respect. I know that there will be times that Nicholas's behavior will not reflect who he truly is and that is okay. That's okay? You may or may not be thinking what kind of parent are you, Shari? A really imperfect, yet intentional, fun, loving, and accountable one. You see while I worked at Nicholas's school I got to better understand that even a child has their own perception of themselves and the world around them. They however can tend to lack understanding of how they should respond in various situations. You see a child knows when their need isn't being met, they just don't know how to always express it.

The times that Nicholas would act outside of himself at school, I would punish the behavior, not him. I would remind him that he is loved, has a powerful mind and I would help him practice sharing his feelings. If you have kids, remember they are learning and you don't want them to believe that they are their behaviors, but instead they can choose new behaviors and still get their needs met. You just have to practice with them and show them how. Let them know that you truly dislike their behavior, but that you still love them. The idea that they should just know you love them, is one that won't serve your relationship with them. Kids don't know what you don't say or show to them. Discover how they best receive information whether visual, auditory, or kinesthetic, and teach them that way. You are their first example, just remember they will do as you do, not as you say. As people, we are constantly thinking and choosing our behaviors. We choose our behaviors based on how we think we will get our needs met.

When you want to fix your behaviors, you can't go straight to the behavior and attack it. This doesn't work because the behavior is driven by a belief, so you must address the underlying belief first. You can do this effectively by first getting into a positive state of mind. When your mind is in a positive state you can process information more objectively.

Here are 10 Ways To Change Your State of Mind Quickly

1. Cold Exposure- Splashing really cold water on your face will give you a boost of energy and help you to reset your mind on something positive.
2. Comedy- Laughter is the best medicine, it can instantly change your mood to a more playful and positive one.

3. Exercise- Any type of exercise is going to get your endorphins going and cause more oxygen to get to your brain which will help you to think clearer.

4. Meditation- Meditation is my favorite! The inner peace you can gain from giving yourself permission to be still is life-changing.

5. Take Long Breaths Out- When we get tense or stressed we tend to hold our breaths in. When you take deep breaths out you get more oxygen to your brain which helps you to manage your brain.

6. Replacing Caffeine With Smoothies- Caffeine will have your mind racing and can easily trigger anxiety. Smoothies packed with healthy nutrients will give you more energy.

7. Supplements- Probiotics are a great supplement for good gut health. Your body is meant to detox toxins. If your gut isn't healthy you will feel extremely sluggish no matter what energy drinks you drink. These will put good bacteria into your body and support your digestion.

8. Journal- This is another favorite. You can become your own best coach by journaling each day. Instead of complaining to others which doesn't truly help you, write down your thoughts in a journal. This frees your mind and helps you to see what you may be in true need of.

9. Worship- Gratitude for all you have, all you are, and all you will become can be done through worship. Play some worship music to instantly shift your state of mind.

10. Reading- A good book, like this one can shift your perspective and place you in a better state of mind.

If you want to produce behaviors that feel good to your soul and get you the results you desire in your life, then you have to become proactive with choosing your state of mind. So if watching the news, listening to drama, or scrolling through social media causes you feelings of worry or anxiety you should limit the time your spending doing those things. What will happen if I do away with those things? You will have more peace of mind which will help you to design a life you're not constantly trying to escape from. That means choosing to intentionally focus your attention on things that place you in the best state of mind. It's not about avoiding life. It's giving yourself time, space, and practice working through your emotions and beliefs so that as life happens you can respond instead of reacting. When you allow external things and people to control your focus you will spend a lot of time reacting to life instead of creating an intentional one.

You also have to take time to identify the pattern of behaviors that you have that keep creating interruptions in your life. Seeking support is not a weakness. I use to think coaching and therapy were really weird and that it couldn't possibly be helpful. I use to think no one could possibly tell me more about myself other than myself. What happens though is that we have biases around ourselves and those biases try to justify our behaviors. Seeking a trusted unbiased person can bring clarity into our lives. So many women put off things like meditation, coaching, therapy, and taking time for self-care and it's not okay. Can I say that again? It's not okay! You should not be okay with not taking care of yourself and giving yourself the emotional tools you need to live a greater quality of life. You should not feel comfortable ignoring your inner cries for help with suppression and excuses. You are a jewel, treat yourself like one. You are a gift, see yourself as one. You hold more value than any external thing you can acquire, so treat yourself well. If you only could see what God sees, when he looks at your beautiful face you would give yourself space and grace to nurture your soul.

CHAPTER 6

Your Spirituality

Spirituality is a personal journey. It is something that cannot and should not be forced on you, it is something you must choose to pursue. I think we all can agree that there is a force beyond ourselves that is at work in the world. I call that force, God. I think we also can agree that there is a power within us that makes us think higher. I call that force, The Holy Spirit. Let me tell you a little about my journey with my spirituality and you can see if there is any part of my story you can relate to.

Where do I begin? I grew up hearing about God. I remember my mom playing gospel music every Sunday and singing to the top of her lungs. We would go to church here and there, but that is all I really knew about God. I remember spending my summers in Jamaica as a young girl and my grandparents would go to church during the week and on Sundays. They attended a Catholic church which was very different from the ones that I went to with my mom. I didn't know much about the differences between different denominations, but I knew how I felt when I heard gospel music. It was the music that drew me closer to God at first. When I would hear the music my soul would feel warm and peace would come over me. When I became old enough to drive and got my first car, I would go to church on Sundays by myself. I was searching for a connection with God. At the time I lived a very reckless lifestyle. I call it reckless because I had no true direction. I wanted certain things in my life, but I wasn't quite sure how to get them. I drank more than I should have, was sexually active, and struggled so much with my self-worth. I spent years living this way, I didn't have bad intentions, I just wanted to feel good about myself. I thought my lifestyle would help me to do that. When I had my son Nicholas, my whole world changed. I was now looking at a reflection of myself in a different form and I didn't want to break his heart. I wanted to be a mom that he would be proud of, I wanted peace in our lives.

One day I remember thinking of trying yoga. I heard that yoga was known for helping you find inner peace, so I was willing to try it. I found a free yoga class at a nearby park, so I went. I was desperate at this point to experience a change in my life and to find out if God was real. I laid on my yoga mat and looked up at the sunny sky. The yoga instructor told us to ask the universe for whatever we needed. I closed my eyes and said, "God. If you are real and if you care about me, please send some women to study the Bible with me." That was it, that was my prayer. After the yoga class ended a group of girls walked over to me and introduced themselves to me. One asked me if I had a church home? I told her I was looking for one that had a children's ministry. Then she invited me to her church and to hang out with her and her friends. Wait! What?? Did this really just happen? I just prayed and here are these girls inviting me to church and to hang out. My mind was blown. The next year and a half I met so many women that studied the Bible with me every week. They made time in their busy schedules just to meet with me. I had never experienced anything like that before. I began growing in my faith and my conviction of who God was. I began seeing miracles and God's promises in real-time. I also began experiencing emotional attacks.

I rededicated my life to Christ and got baptized. I became a new creature in Christ. My heart was different, my desires started to change. It wasn't me, it was God's love that left me wanting more of him. I didn't fall in love with God by way of religion or tradition. It was through a relationship. I can't tell you how many nights I have cried out to God to ease the pains of my mind and he would rescue me. I can't tell you the bold decisions he has encouraged me to take that have changed my whole life. Before I had an active relationship with God, I struggled with fear and allowed it to hold me captive. Now I realize that fear and courage can coexist. Something started to change as I grew closer to God, I started to develop faith. Faith is the substance of things you can not see. You see when you start growing in faith, you stop entertaining conversations of doubt. When you start growing in faith, you stop letting people place their own limitations on you. When you start growing in faith you realize that everything is working for your good. What do you think of when you think of God?

I pray that the flaws of Christians don't push you away from knowing God's unmatched character. God is not like people, he is perfectly just. I can try to share all my love with you, but even all my love won't match one moment in God's presence. You are a spirit being having a human experience and your soul will always yearn for a deeper connection than the ones you have with people. I don't force my beliefs on people, I don't have to. God is bigger than everything. Once you are ready to find him, I trust you will and I know you will experience his power in your life. Religion is about man-made rules, I don't believe in religion. I do believe in having a relationship with God. When you develop a relationship with God you don't have to worry about being perfect, his love will perfect your faith throughout your lifetime. No striving, no guilt or shame, just you and him.

Spirituality is a lifelong journey. We will always find ourselves seeking, learning, and growing in our understanding. I don't know where you are in your journey, but I do know that God loves you. He is crazy about you, so much that he sent Jesus to die on a cross just so your sins would be forgiven. He wanted to show his deep love for you, by having his son die, then be raised back to life again. He wanted to show you that not even death could overcome you. How does it feel to know that he watches over you? How does it feel to know that he has a plan for your life? You don't need a fancy outfit or to look a certain way to be close to him. You don't need to be any way other than who you are right now in this moment. God knows the real you, not the you that you have perfected presenting in order for people to like you. God sees your true heart and says you are worth every ounce of his love. In the darkest seasons of your life, he will find you and bring you into his light. Talk to him, like I did. Let him know your fears like I did. Ask him to show you that he is real and he will. Don't allow people to dictate who God is for you, seek him for yourself.

What was your introduction to faith?

Was your introduction to faith patient, kind, unconditional?

How would your life be different if you believed God loved you no matter what you did or how you feel about him?

My spirit feels secure, calm, and peaceful when I am doing:

CHAPTER 7

Your Grief

Watching the people you love die too soon, is a pain like no other. It causes you to question many things. It begins to rock your concept of what is certain and forces you to face the feelings that uncertainty brings. Having to ask yourself questions isn't a bad thing and I have found that the right questions can lead you to find peace. My first experience with grief was losing my mother to cancer. Never would I have imagined losing my mom at the age of 21. Moms are supposed to live till their 90 or at least that was what I believed. It all happened so fast. I started to notice one day that her skin looked yellow. My mom kept everything from me, I am sure she thought she was protecting me. I remember dropping her off at the doctor's office, not knowing what was going on. Eventually, she told me she was doing treatments, but I didn't know she was having chemo treatments. The truth is her being so secretive about it made me feel afraid to ask. I remember her spending a month or so in the hospital. When she finally came back home I remember her eventually functioning like she normally would. It wasn't that long though before she was sick again, this time I could tell something was really wrong. My mom and dad didn't have the best relationship and she would share small details with me. Watching her battle for her life and knowing that she was struggling in her marriage broke my heart. In fact, it made me angry.

I held a lot of resentment towards my father because I thought that maybe if she was happy she wouldn't have gotten sick. I know it wasn't my father's fault and I know it pained him to see her in so much pain. I remember one day standing in the foyer and my mom started hugging me and crying saying, " I don't want to die." I hugged her tight and just cried. I still had no idea at this point that she had cancer, but I could see the pain in her eyes. It all went downhill very fast from there. She got sicker and sicker and I was still too afraid to ask. I would try to be helpful and ask her what she needed, but she still tried to be strong.

My mom was a special woman, I only wish she knew how special she truly was. I wish she knew that her strength wasn't in how much she could endure and that transparency offers a sweet gift to those that lean into it. A different kind of healing takes place when you allow those that love you to help you carry the load when it gets too heavy. I only wish she had given me a chance to really be there for her. I imagine she was doing what generations before her had done, which was to fight in silence with hopes that she would shield those closest to her from the pain. Pain isn't always our enemy, I have learned it to be a teacher. I only wish we could have learned together. My mom ended up in hospice. I will never forget going to visit her and having to prepare my mind each time I left to never see her again. I was working for the airlines at the time. I still remember the day she passed. I was working and I told a friend of mine at work that my mom was in hospice. He prayed with me. I knew I was going to see her after work, but this time I had peace in my soul. It was as if God had prepared me for that day. I got to the hospice and I asked everyone that was in the room to give me a moment alone with her. I told her how much I loved her. I told her that I would look out for my brother, I told her I would become all she ever dreamed and I told her that I would one day make up with my dad. She wanted me to have a relationship with my dad. After I shared my heart with her, she took her final breath. It was like she had waited for me. I kissed her cold face and I said goodbye. That was one of the deepest heartbreaks of my life. Who was going to teach me how to be a woman? Who was going to walk through pregnancy with me? Who would I call when my heart was broken? Who would tell me that I would make a beautiful bride? I had so much more to learn about life, who was going to teach me? I still wish I had more time to love her. I wish I could hug and kiss her beautiful face. I wish she could be a part of the love that I share with Nicholas every day.

There came a time when I decided to release the burden of guilt I felt for not doing or saying more while she was alive. I believe the best gift I could give her is to live my life filled with hope, joy, and love for others. I didn't know then what I know now. I didn't have the bold faith then, that I do now. I became the woman I am today because the impact of her loss led me to discover myself. She had planted enough seeds in my life that led me straight to God. I was blessed to have her as my mom and I know she felt blessed to have me too. I see her smile and I hear her laugh every time I think of her. I know she is overjoyed to know that I have a relationship with my dad and that I never stopped looking out for my brother. I know she is proud of me and that is all the closure I will ever need.

Grief isn't the same for any of us. It shouldn't be compared. Grief isn't limited to losing a loved one, you can grieve anything that once held significance in your heart. Grief has stages and some stages last longer than others. Learning the different stages of grief can help you to understand that all the feelings you may be having are okay. You may experience feelings of denial, guilt, anger, depression, envy, or yearning after losing someone or something you deeply love. It is okay to struggle through grief. It is okay to have moments of laughter then shortly after feel moments of frustration. It is okay to reach out for support or to feel in moments that you can't manage the presence of others. Having support isn't about taking the pain away, it's about having a safe space to unravel and regain your strength. Space where you won't be taken advantage of in your vulnerability.

This was a tough moment in my life that turned out to be a powerful "purpose pivot". To me, a purpose pivot is a moment in your life that hurts like crazy but shows you that you have so much more to give because you survived it. If the moment wasn't working for your good, then you wouldn't have made it through. These moments grow you in compassion and empathy so that you can extend yourself to other people that will one day feel those same hurts.

Losing my mom wasn't my last run-in with grief. In 2020 and 2021 my heart was broken not once, but twice. I had two stillbirths, one with my daughter Grace and the other my son Mateo.

From my journal:

I had dreams of my daughter, Grace Glory Green. She was so active inside my stomach. I use to joke and say she was having worship practice or preparing a word that she would share with her kindergarten class one day. I wanted so badly the chance to build a mother-daughter relationship with her and to teach her all that took me years to discover. What I never dreamed of was bringing her into this world only to have to send her back to be with God. It's hard as a mother to find peace and not to recount it all trying to find something you should have done differently. To know that God formed her in my womb, made her in his image, gave her a purpose, but has a plan for her life that doesn't involve me walking beside her is tough to understand.

So the question I ask myself daily and sometimes feel pushed to face by others unknowingly is what's next? Some say "You look good, you must be well." Not knowing some days I struggle to look anything other than how I feel. Some say "You're so strong." They don't know that I am doing what my bible tells me to do and that is to allow God to meet me in the depths of my weakness, so he can be my strength. Some say, "No worries. Soon you'll have a rainbow baby." Not knowing that while God can give me another baby, they won't be Grace.

So I stopped searching for my own understanding of my next steps and I asked God to give me wisdom. He first pointed out that Grace is my rainbow. He didn't fail on his promise to me. I got to see her sweet face, hold her, watch my husband read to her, and it was beautiful. Some things in me changed during those 8 months of carrying her. My endurance grew through what wasn't an easy pregnancy. I was sick most of it. Even when I felt miserable, I found I still had enough love inside me to give away to others. Everything I have poured out has come back to me and my family during this time 10 times over. Grace we miss you, love you, and will keep you with us in our hearts.

My next journal entry was a familiar one that had evolved in its meaning.

On Jan 2, 2021, I felt a familiar feeling that something was wrong. My sweet baby Mateo had stopped moving. As I began preparing my heart for what I had experienced only 9 months before with sweet baby Grace, I decided not to even try to accept it in my own strength but to give my fragile heart back to God.

This time around experiencing loss was familiar but different in many ways. There was a familiar pain and deep sadness, but there was a tremendous strength that I couldn't even understand that was present.

This time when the doctor and nurses told me there was no heartbeat, peace came over me. The first thing out of my mouth was "Do you guys know Jesus and how much he loves you?" In the midst of my tragedy, God placed it in my heart to share his love for them with them. My next concern was how I was going to tell my son Nicholas. We had all been telling him how lucky Mateo was to have him as a big brother and how lucky we were to have Mateo.

Again God reminded me that the same strength he gives us, he gives to all his children. Even the little ones. I didn't even get my whole speech of "comfort" out to Nicholas before he said " Now that Mateo is in heaven, Grace doesn't have to be alone. It's a good thing." My faith grew in that moment! Wheeew.

The day before my induction God told me to host a bible study with my immediate and extended family. My heart still jumps when I think of all the faces on the zoom call and all God did that evening that I knew of and may never know. Seeds were sown in all our lives, that God will be sure to bless.

The induction, delivery, and birth were all filled with God's provision, love, familiar faces, and peace. I realized I was only experiencing something God had gone ahead to prepare for me. I realized how much he loved me. After a short labor Mateo was born.

The day we spent with Mateo was beautiful, we even had a baptism that was so special.

A loss only remains a loss when you stop the story. My loss is no longer because what I gained has begun a new chapter in my story. So Grace & Mateo are not lost but with the best caretaker, I could have chosen for them. They are the very sweet souls that helped increase my faith and give me purpose to live beyond my comfort zone. They have connected me to people, I would have never met.

Grace taught me to give GRACE. Mateo taught me that life itself is a GIFT. Both times I have had the pleasure of seeing the quiet strength of my husband. I admire the man that he is, how he cares for me and I wouldn't want to walk in the wilderness with anyone else.

What I want you to remember the most is that life will bring tough feelings and experiences your way. After losing my sweet babies I had to learn how to grieve beside my husband. We didn't grieve the same way but we allowed for each other's form of grief to be okay. Working through our grief made our marriage stronger. There are parts of yourself that must develop by way of testing. Your grief isn't meant to hurt you or to remove love from your life. I know it may feel like it is, but it only reveals how much value your life has been filled with. It gives you a deeper appreciation for the people and things you still have. There are parts of grief that you must learn to surrender to God because only he knows truly understands the why behind your loss. Take your tears, frustration, and all your emotions to him he can handle them all. Remember he knows you and loves you as you are. In time you will better understand the meaning in all you have experienced. You will learn his promise may not be the thing you want but it will be the thing you need when it comes to pass. You will grow in compassion. You will find restoration. You will still have moments where your feelings won't match your faith. That's okay, he will be there for that too. Just know that he will never leave you, nor forsake you. Just know that God's love always has been and always will be enough to cover you in whatever season you are in.

What would grief be like if you didn't judge your feelings?

What is the worst that can happen if you allow yourself to feel your feelings?

What is the best possible outcome if you gave yourself time and space to explore your grief?

CHAPTER 8

Your Relationships

Life is all about relationships. The relationships you choose to cultivate will either add value to your life or greatly distract you. Now relationships aren't by any means perfect, but there should be a perfected purpose that you see as the relationship matures. So choose wisely. You have the right to decide the level of access you allow people to have in your life. Choosing a relationship should be done with consideration of shared values, not shared personalities. Would you want to date someone that was exactly like you? Your dope but let's be honest there are some ways that you have that would be complemented by someone with a different personality type. The relationship you have with yourself is mirrored in all your relationships in every season of your life. The relationship you have with yourself affects every other relationship you will ever have. If you find yourself attracting relationships that lead to trauma and confusion, you should pause and ask yourself whether or not you have connected with them for the right reasons. Find out what that connection is trying to teach about where you currently are. The degree to which you can connect and understand yourself is the degree you will be able to connect with others. The traits you notice in others good or bad at some level exist within you. If it didn't you wouldn't be able to identify it, that is why self-awareness is so important.

What conversations are you having in your mind about you? Are you hyping yourself up?! Or are you constantly criticizing your every move? Once we have more self-acceptance then we become more accepting of others. Self-acceptance is extremely important because there will be seasons in your life where you may find yourself in a different season than those closest to you. It is important that you learn to anchor yourself in the emotions that are most encouraging for you no matter what emotions those around you may be experiencing. Remember earlier I shared that in N.L.P, we say "the map is not the territory." In your relationships, your goal is not to place your map onto the other person but to respect where they are as you both grow into the relationship you desire to have. You can always influence those around you by the energy you choose to hold each day. I know we live in a culture that quickly cancels people, but throwing people away won't fix the things that need to be worked out in your heart. There are circumstances where a season of a relationship is up, but for the ones that are meant to stick around you have to learn how to work through your differences.

Let's start with the relationship you have with yourself. Oftentimes, we feel all sorts of internal discomforts as women and instead of dealing with them, we look for external fixes. It may feel good for a moment, but then those discomforts come back stronger. Have you ever blown up on someone and then hours later thought to yourself, I may have overreacted. I have my hand raised! Unresolved traumas and emotions can cause us to destroy what God called us to help build in our relationships. Unresolved issues can have us trying to fix others while neglecting the work we should be doing within ourselves. In the 30 day exercise in the book, I am going to teach you how to start coaching yourself so that you can find daily relief for your frustrations.

I have discovered from talking with several women that there are 3 main thoughts that keep women from living with inner peace.

1. **I am not enough.**

Do you feel good enough?

Think as far back as you can to your childhood. Your parents, caretakers, teachers, and the people you admired either affirmed you, or maybe they didn't. We look to those we trust for affirmation of our worthiness. When we experience constant rejection, it affects our self-esteem. We then become extra careful with how we "come off" out of fear that we will experience that same rejection again or become extra aggressive to feel in control. It could also look like detaching ourselves from others to avoid conflict because we don't want to feel any pain. We can even experience behaviors like people-pleasing, codependency, and living on high alert. So how do you shift how you experience rejection? Understand that rejection is just redirection. Rejection is not an emergency, although it may feel like one on the inside. Everything is happening for you! Yes, even the tension in your relationships is happening for you. They are showing you areas of your heart that still need work. So when things or people don't respond in your favor that is an opportunity to realign yourself with the right things or to repair your relationships. Repairing can be done through the speaker/listener technique. One person speaks. The other person repeats what they heard. The speaker confirms or brings more clarity to the conversation. Then you switch roles. It's an opportunity to gain understanding, not to cast shame or blame.

2. What I want is not available to me.

Have you ever looked at someone's life and thought man they are so lucky?

When we compare our lives to others we miss out on the beauty in our own lives. We each have our own struggles to grow through and while you may not see the struggles of others, they do exist. The shift begins when you start to place your attention on the significant things in your life. That means consuming more of what builds you up personally. When you start to worry more than being present, it creates feelings of anxiety and depression. If you were listening to your favorite song, but the whole time you were thinking of why God didn't give you a voice like Beyonce, then you would miss out on the beauty of your favorite song. If you spend all your time focusing on what others are doing, your mind will continue to compare itself against what it sees. Start to create small daily goals for yourself and track them. Start to write down what you admire about yourself. What this will do is build your confidence in achieving what is meaningful to you. The more evidence you see, the more you will realize that what you desire is not just available to you, but you had access to it all along.

3. I'm different from everyone else, I'm not special.

Have you ever been in a crowd and thought no one looks or thinks like me?

Sometimes your natural desire for connection pushes you to look for familiarity in order to feel accepted. God called you to serve the crowd, not to be like the crowd. The moment you accept this is the moment you will start showing up more as yourself no matter where you are. To think that your quirks and personality are not good enough is to think that God made an error when he made you. We know that isn't even possible. Wanna know a secret? Everyone truly admires people who are comfortable just being themselves. So the more you practice it, the more comfortable you will feel. You will notice yourself creating a greater level of impact in the lives around you.

Let's look at what happens in our romantic relationships. What we often think when thinking of finding love is gaining more of everything we desire and love. This can be a reality, but the truest reality is that not only do you have your own set of desires so does your partner. Blending two sets of expectations while navigating each other's fears is the part that takes practice but can be done. You both hold the same fear which is the fear of what life will be like and feel like if your pictured expectation isn't met. Both people have created this picture in their head of what a good life looks like and letting go of that picture is what creates tension, until you learn that you can create a new picture that is bigger and brighter together.

We carry a story in our romantic relationships too. If you are telling yourself that your husband doesn't really listen to you or value your opinions then guess what you're going to find more evidence of? You're going to pick the few moments where he isn't listening to you, to confirm your story in your head. Remember what we focus on grows and we choose what we want to focus on, it's not the other way around. It took me getting married to learn that most of what I had assumed and been taught about marriage was wrong. You don't just meet the perfect man and then it's happily ever after. If you're signing up to be in a relationship, you are signing up to put in work. You are signing up to grow into the marriage of your dreams. Marriage is filled with fun and is truly the safest relationship you can be in when both people are committed to it working. Have you ever thought things would be so much easier if he would just... Yeah. Your going to be miserable if that is what you are waiting on. So I am going to teach you how to manage your relationship like the queen you are, without needing to change him. These strategies can be used in all of your relationships.

1. **Speaker Listener Technique**- the only reason you don't get along with someone is that you have fallen out of rapport with them. You can establish rapport using this technique. One person tells the other how they feel, while the other just listens. The person listening repeats what they heard the speaker saying. The goal is for the listener to gain understanding and for the speaker to feel validation in being understood. Once the speaker confirms being understood you switch roles and repeat. This gives both people a chance to understand and affirm how each other is feeling.

2. **Attack the issue**- people get offended when they feel that you are attacking their intention. No one wants to feel misunderstood. You shouldn't accuse someone of having a certain intention because you are not in their mind, so you don't truly know what they were thinking. You can share how their behavior made you feel. Say "I want to spend more quality time with you." Instead of, "You don't care about me, you're always on your phone." Attack the issue, not the person. If you need to vent, call a time out, or share your raw feelings in a journal before you share with them. Decide how you can address the issue together without labeling each other as the problem. Remember you are two people having a problem, you each are not a problem. Focus on finding the solution. Try not to discuss hard topics late at night, wait until your wide awake and calm.

3. **Give them their love language**- Find out if their love language is physical touch, words of affirmation, gifts, quality time, or acts of service. Make time daily to show each other your love languages.

4. **Create new expectations**- You both came into the relationship with expectations but now you have to create new ones that support your life together. You both will experience fear around letting go of some of your expectations, so show each other grace as you learn to adapt. Spend time dreaming together. Shared goals and dreams help you to stay connected throughout different phases of your relationship. Create a shared vision for what you both want your relationship to look and feel like.

5. **Learn when you should speak**- Your words hold power and learning when they are most helpful will save you a lot of unnecessary arguments. Ask yourself If what you want to say will be helpful at that moment? Nagging won't get you what you truly want, effective communication will.

What your going to find is that you will get more of the results you want to see, without needing to change the person. The way you see your partner and conflict will begin to change and you will see yourself showing up confidently in your relationship. You will learn that you no longer have to match his energy, instead, you can take responsibility for maintaining the energy you desire to have. You will also notice him changing on his own. You have to accept that your partner's behavior is not who they are and is not your fault. The behaviors he shows are the ones that he chooses based on his state of mind. Get to understand his state of mind and you will understand his behavior. This can be applied to your relationship with your kids and friends.

Now one thing you may wish you could avoid but you can't is conflict. If you change how you see and deal with conflict, your conflicts will start to look a lot different. When someone does something that makes you upset, ask yourself which one of their basic needs were they trying to fulfill? Their behavior isn't about you remember, it's about them meeting their needs. Unfortunately how we each choose to meet our needs at times can be hurtful to others. When you take time to gain understanding, then you can address the issue not them, you are going to see them be more receptive to fixing what your asking of them.

Let's first talk about how we each prefer to receive love and information. There are three ways that all human beings receive information visual, auditory, and kinesthetic. After I teach you this, you are going to be more aware of this happening during your conversations. People who are more visual are going to need a visual representation. So if you can show them a visual of what you are saying, it will be more helpful. Recalling a previous experience can also be helpful. Say you ask your husband to go to the store to pick up your favorite milk. If he has never seen your favorite milk and picked it up himself before, he will probably ask you to send him a picture of it. You may be thinking, I told him the name of it before and he sees me drink it all the time. If his mind is struggling to find an image of the milk, it will be more frustrating for him to find the milk without a picture. People who are visual will talk with more descriptive words to help build for you the picture they see in their minds. Auditory learners are different. You can give them step-by-step instructions or details and they will be able to remember. They also will be able to remember exactly what you said that hurt them or made them feel loved.

Kinesthetic learners are very hands-on and are usually more touchy-feely. The thing is that we all can receive information and love in all of these ways but, we may prefer to receive some ways more than others. Have you ever had a disagreement with someone and instead of them verbally apologizing, they gave you a hug. The hug probably didn't feel comforting to you, if you are more of an auditory receiver. Hearing them be remorseful would feel well to you. However, they may have been kinesthetic receivers which is why they thought you would like the hug. This happens every day in our relationships. We tend to love others, how we truly desire to be loved. If we want to have fulfilling relationships we have to learn to give others what feels good to them. If your mind is thinking, they are going to get whatever I give, then you need to unpack why you think people should only receive whatever your willing to give them. Is everyone not worthy of being loved how they best feel loved?

If you have children the same strategy applies. Do you know one of the greatest gifts you can give children? The gift of not trying to fix everything. No child wants to feel like everything they do is wrong and that your way is always the better way. This robs them of learning and their need for autonomy. There are times when your comfort doesn't need to look like fixing. Sometimes comfort looks like giving them space to sit with their emotions. Sometimes comfort looks like not judging their emotions. Sometimes comfort looks like letting them know even with their emotions, your there and you love them. Don't forget that your children are human beings too with needs and feelings. You are helping them learn how to regulate their own emotions by the ways you respond.

Your need to fix everything is about you. Maybe fixing makes you feel significant, but is it the most beneficial to those you are trying to fix? It is okay to ask them what would be helpful for them at that moment and to allow them to process what they actually need from you. This gives them a chance to process and eventually learn to think about what they may need regularly. Obviously, there are age-appropriate responses that speak to your child's individual needs. Just remember that in order for them to learn and master anything, they need opportunities to practice. What would your parenting look like if you stopped trying to make your child into who you think they should be and you instead gracefully guided them into who God created them to be? Nothing compares to the love you get to share with those close to you. You were created for connection with others. Your quality of life is greatly tied to the quality of communication you have with those around you. You have everything you need to cultivate the relationships you truly desire, you deserve to have them.

Are your relationships based on shared values and expectations?

What qualities do you see in your relationships that let you know that they are healthy? What qualities do you see that let you know they need work?

Do your relationships have boundaries? What are they?

Relationship Cycles

Every relationship has its own cycle look at the example and see if you can identify with it.

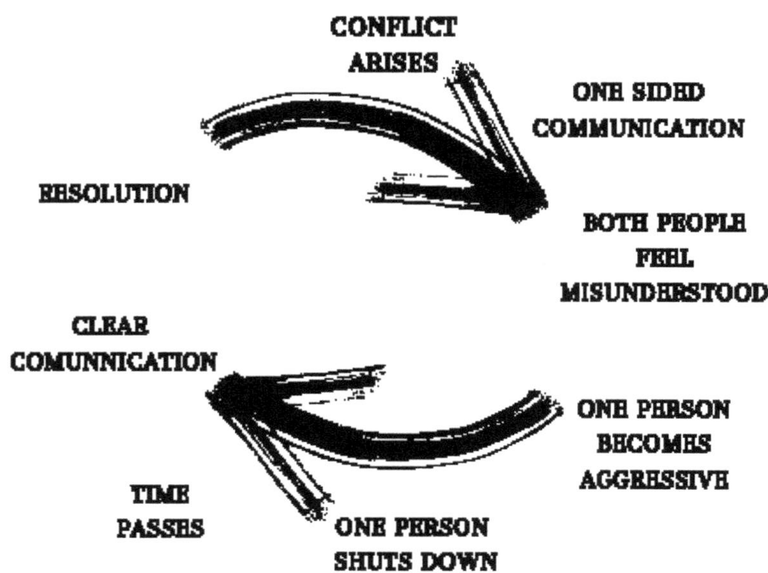

Every relationship has a cycle that causes a breakdown in communication. I want you to think of your closest relationships and what happens within your communication that may cause breakdowns. Once you identify the cycles that currently exist you can create exit strategies that lead to a new way of managing conflict. Conflict is not bad, it should be expected. When you have two people with their own biases and maps of the world there are sure to be misunderstandings. If you struggle with accepting conflict as a natural experience it could be because you saw it handled in a harmful way and the thought of facing it scares you. Remember you have more resources now that you can use to navigate tough conversations with more grace than you may have seen.

From looking at the example what do you think the first exit strategy could be? When you are addressing conflict the very first thing you want to do is to pause if there seems to be a breakdown in communication. If you notice a lack of understanding around what the real issue is then there is no reason to move ahead, just stop!

Use these steps

1. Get clarity on the real issue. (Don't move from finding the real issue until you discover what is. Ask questions instead of making assumptions.)
2. Affirm how the real issue has affected both people.
3. Reaffirm your love for your relationship
4. Work to create a solution together. (Ex. How could we have handled this better? How can we handle this in the future?)

You may have to be the first one to introduce this new way of handling conflict and that is okay. Don't get discouraged if things don't change right away or if your old way of handling conflict comes back up. You stick to managing your own emotions and set an example. It will take time and practice but you will see that it works. How important are your relationships to you? They should mean more to you than always being right. They should reflect the direction of your purpose.

CHAPTER 9

Your Purpose

You have probably spent most of your life focused on what you think others would approve of in your life. You have probably spent more time doing that instead of mastering the gifts God has given you. You have probably compared yourself to other women more than you have acknowledged just how amazing you are. Why is that? You have been taught unconsciously to strive to be like or better than others. Tell me this though, if you are busy being like others when will the world get the gift of meeting you? Not the person you chose to hide behind, the real authentic you. Do you think God created you to be limited by the opinions of others? Your purpose is to live out the will God has planned for your life. It isn't something you go looking for. It is something you discover through living with intention. Are you driven by money or the impact you know you have the capacity to create? The more present you become with yourself, the more your purpose will be revealed to you through the spirit of God within you. Find the courage to get still. What do you mean? I mean for once in your life spend some time not worrying about the things around you and start listening to the voice within you.

I mentioned that your purpose was to live out God's will for your life but what I didn't mention was that you have your own free will. The human will is the most powerful thing on earth because not even God can control it. This means that even though God has constructed a perfect plan for you, you can still choose not to follow it. Your will is yours which can be a precious or a dangerous gift. You have been given a gift that can be used to reject the one who gave it to you. Your will lives in your heart. You have two minds. You have a conscious mind and an unconscious mind. Cognitive neuroscientists have said that our decisions, thoughts, behaviors, and feelings are created 95% of the time from the unconscious part of our minds. So we are only conscious of all those things 5% of the time. Your heart is guided by your unconscious mind. That is where your deepest beliefs are stored. The more your conscious mind hears something it feeds it to your unconscious mind. Your mind is the center of all your thoughts. You become what you are constantly hearing and thinking. Begin feeding your mind what you desire to live out in your life.

Remind yourself that you don't need a feeling to validate you moving in the direction of your purpose you just need a revelation of what direction you need to be heading in. Did you know you can do things afraid? You don't need to always feel 100% certain to do something. Think of when you are driving. You aren't certain that a crazy driver won't cross into your lane causing an accident. Yet you still turn up your favorite song and have your own private concert not worrying about a soul. Your faith in one area can be transferred to any other area of your life. You can't possibly think God created you to simply exist, pay bills, lose weight, and eat your feelings away. You are far more valuable than you know. Your purpose is not something you find by worrying about it, it is something you discover by taking action. Have you ever found yourself constantly asking God to give you something to do? Your waiting for him to give you this big monumental assignment but you still haven't done the first thing he instructed you to do years ago?

What can you do right now with your time and gifts to be a blessing to someone else? If you don't have money guess what you do have creativity and time. If you don't have time guess what you have creativity and money. If you don't have time or money guess what you do have, creativity and discipline. You can never lack what you need to live your purpose because your main purpose in life is to serve others out of the abundance of what God gives you.

Purpose is not an event, it is an ongoing revealing of your highest potential and the meanings attached to every experience. Purpose is that thing you feel you should be doing that scares you. It becomes easy to recognize because when you see others doing it, it stirs up something within you. When you see others flowing in it, you say I should be doing that. So why haven't you started yet? Why are you not doing that thing? Why can't you see that your ability to identify with it is only because it exists within you on some level? Purpose is wrapped up in your soapbox. Your soapbox is the arena of life that you can talk about, advocate for, and create solutions for all day, every day because it means that much to you. Many of us discover our purpose through our painful moments. You are wondering why life has dealt you certain experiences, but the wisdom you have gained could save lives if you would only share it. It is not enough to just identify your purpose, you must learn how to focus on it. Before you can know where to focus you must first have a vision.

If you have no vision, you will focus on all the wrong things in life. "Walk by faith, not by sight " (2 Corinthians 5:7.) If you only live by what you see, you will constantly create excuses to not live from a space of abundance. Or you can find yourself so distracted with trying to fix others so much so that you neglect rescuing yourself first. I had a conversation once with a potential client and she mentioned that she wanted to make some changes in her life. I started asking her questions to see if she was ready for the changes and I realized she wasn't. You see the reason why a lot of people won't become who they want to be is that they are too attached to who they have been. They know that who they have been is no longer working for them but, they haven't discovered a clear enough vision yet to make that change. I remember all the changes I personally had to start making to transition into coaching. There were moments when it felt hard but then I realized I had already overcome some of the hardest challenges of my life. The "hard" only existed in my mind. I started trying to distract myself by doing things for others. I learned that you can't try to carry everyone with you when you are making significant changes in your life. I had to rescue myself, learn myself, teach myself before I could even try to rescue anyone else. I am much more valuable to my family and community now because I was willing to do the hard work within myself.

Do you know what happens when you have no clear vision? You get degrees you never use, you take jobs you dread going to and you live with a scarcity mindset. It may be what you saw your parents do. You learned how to survive, instead of how to live intentionally. You learned to see yourself as a servant and not the leader you are. You are a leader and every day you are influencing those that watch and listen to you. Let them see you taking time to care for yourself.

To focus means to aim to reach a specific destination. What do you think happens to women filled with gifts, but void of vision? They travel life filled with potential, regret, restlessness, and resentment. Is that a life you're willing to settle for? If you aim everywhere, you will end up hitting nothing. The reason so many of us struggle with anxiety and depression is that we are busy being busy and not focused on getting to a specific destination. Focusing on the past leads to depression because there is no undoing what has already been done. Focusing on the future creates anxiety because your experiences may limit how you think God will move in your life. Imagine if you were to call up your girlfriend to meet her for lunch and you asked her where she wanted to go and she said anywhere. You ask her what time she wants to meet and she says anytime. You ask her what day should you two meet and she says any day. When do you think you two will meet? More than likely you two won't end up meeting for another month or even a year. A clear vision is important. If you know what you want it becomes easier to say no to what you don't want.

When you desire a change it can feel really normal to look to others. I think looking to others can help you to learn but remember the goal is not to become them. You are special and what you hold inside you is just as valuable as anyone else you see. Release your obsession with the "how" and become obsessed with your "why." You have given your fears much more time than they deserve.

What do you feel your purpose is?

How can you use your current gifts and talents to serve others?

What drives and motivates you in life?

What do you hope to gain from the things you are doing in your life now?

CHAPTER 10

H.E.A.L Strategy

There are different levels to your healing. Have you ever noticed that you experience new levels of awareness when you are outside of the environment that caused your trauma and pain? You won't be able to truly experience the deep inner healing until your environment becomes conducive for that healing. This is why seasons of isolation and moments of reflection are so important and become powerful when you use them to finally focus on being present with your internal needs. Feelings are not good or bad, they just are. They are signals that are pointing you in the direction of what you need in order to get into alignment with the peaceful version of who you are. We were not created to be ungrateful, anxious, resentful, insecure, numb and so many other feelings we all experience at times. We experience those things because of the imperfections of the world. We each operate at our own levels of awareness, which is why we experience conflict. Once we become exposed to something beyond our current state of mind and take action, transformation takes place. Life gets brighter. Your mind and body are teaching you through your discomforts what you need in order to grow. Can't you see it is working for you?

I have been doing the inner work within myself for years and every year I discover parts of myself that need a new level of awareness. I have accepted that my entire life will revolve around growth. This strategy that I have developed is what has helped me to overcome tough experiences and emotions throughout my life. Feelings aren't good or bad, they just are. This strategy is what you will practice for the next 30 days guaranteeing you more peace in your mind. 95% of your thoughts and behaviors are unconscious. I want you to bring awareness to your past experiences, not to hold you there, but to help you understand how they have shaped where you are in life now. Beliefs can be chosen, unchosen, and evolve in their meanings. So the more time you spend getting acquainted with the meanings attached to your feelings and beliefs, the more conscious you will become in choosing your thoughts and actions.

Hear your story

Express your feelings

Affirm what is true

Live actively with your new-found understanding

Hear your story

Listen to your thoughts sis! What story are you traveling with throughout your day? What are you telling yourself is available to you? What assumptions are you making of other people's actions? Are you assuming everyone views the world as you do? The story you tell yourself every day affects your state of mind. Start your morning by deciding what story you want to carry with you.

Express your feelings

What are you feeling? What happened that changed your state of mind?

Taking time to understand which one of your basic needs feels threatened is going to help you realize which emotional resources you need at that moment. You are no longer a helpless child, you now know that your feelings are only signals. Find out what your feelings are trying to tell you so you can seek relief.

Affirm what is true

It is you who chooses your thoughts. What thoughts can you hold for your highest good? Stop affirming lies and insecurities in your mind. Reframe what is happening to you.

Ex of Reframing: What is happening to me is showing me what no longer works for me and what I now need. I am better for having this experience.

Live actively with your new-found understanding

Now that you have gained a new understanding of what you are experiencing what new behaviors and beliefs will you hold moving forward. Once you have proven something to be a lie you now have to take a new action that reflects your new understanding. Action is where the transformation takes root in your mind.

CHAPTER 11

Day 1

(Fill in the blanks)

This morning I feel :

Today I will focus on :

I feel the most loved and like my life when I am doing :

Today I had to deal with :

What are my feelings on what I had to deal with today? What was the real issue? Did I carry any biases about myself or others?

Which one of my basic needs felt threatened?

How can I reframe what I dealt with today? What was it teaching me?

What kind of support do I need to move past this?

Do I need some time alone or do I need to practice the speaker/listener technique with someone?

Nightly Mantra :

Today I did my best. Today I was enough. Today God was watching over me. I gave myself permission to feel and it was worth it. I am in control of my thoughts and my life. When other people hurt me I have the power to tell them how what they did made me feel. I have the power to decide what no longer serves me and I will release it with ease. I can do things that feel hard. Everything I need is available to me. I am in the process of healing. Today I learned more about who I want to be and what I want in my life. My purpose was created just for me. I will use my gifts and talents to serve now as I grow in my purpose. My heart is growing. I am grateful because I am learning what it means to love, honor, and see me.

Day 2

(Fill in the blanks)

This morning I feel :

Today I will focus on :

I feel the most loved and like my life when I am doing :

Today I had to deal with :

What are my feelings on what I had to deal with today? What was the real issue? Did I carry any biases about myself or others?

Which one of my basic needs felt threatened?

How can I reframe what I dealt with today? What was it teaching me?

What kind of support do I need to move past this?

Do I need some time alone or do I need to practice the speaker/ listener technique with someone?

Nightly Mantra :

Today I did my best. Today I was enough. Today God was watching over me. I gave myself permission to feel and it was worth it. I am in control of my thoughts and my life. When other people hurt me I have the power to tell them how what they did made me feel. I have the power to decide what no longer serves me and I will release it with ease. I can do things that feel hard. Everything I need is available to me. I am in the process of healing. Today I learned more about who I want to be and what I want in my life. My purpose was created just for me. I will use my gifts and talents to serve now as I grow in my purpose. My heart is growing. I am grateful because I am learning what it means to love, honor, and see me.

CHAPTER 13

Day 3

(Fill in the blanks)

This morning I feel :

Today I will focus on :

I feel the most loved and like my life when I am doing :

Today I had to deal with :

What are my feelings on what I had to deal with today? What was the real issue? Did I carry any biases about myself or others?

Which one of my basic needs felt threatened?

How can I reframe what I dealt with today? What was it teaching me?

What kind of support do I need to move past this?

Do I need some time alone or do I need to practice the speaker/ listener technique with someone?

Nightly Mantra :

Today I did my best. Today I was enough. Today God was watching over me. I gave myself permission to feel and it was worth it. I am in control of my thoughts and my life. When other people hurt me I have the power to tell them how what they did made me feel. I have the power to decide what no longer serves me and I will release it with ease. I can do things that feel hard. Everything I need is available to me. I am in the process of healing. Today I learned more about who I want to be and what I want in my life. My purpose was created just for me. I will use my gifts and talents to serve now as I grow in my purpose. My heart is growing. I am grateful because I am learning what it means to love, honor, and see me.

CHAPTER 14

Day 4

(Fill in the blanks)

This morning I feel :

Today I will focus on :

I feel the most loved and like my life when I am doing :

Today I had to deal with :

What are my feelings on what I had to deal with today? What was the real issue? Did I carry any biases about myself or others?

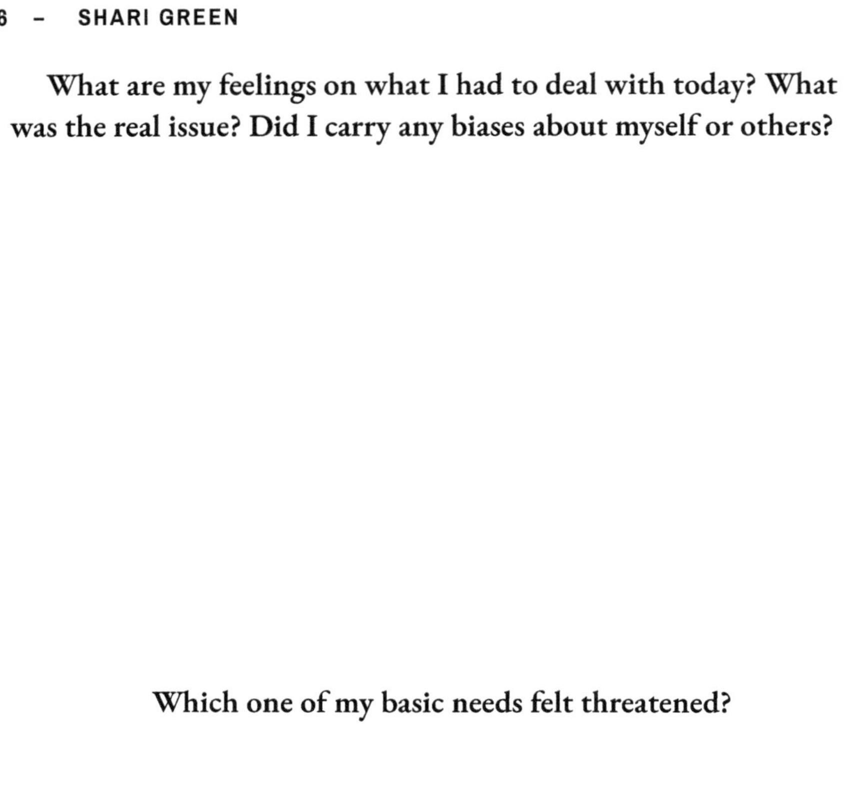

Which one of my basic needs felt threatened?

How can I reframe what I dealt with today? What was it teaching me?

What kind of support do I need to move past this?

Do I need some time alone or do I need to practice the speaker/ listener technique with someone?

Nightly Mantra :

Today I did my best. Today I was enough. Today God was watching over me. I gave myself permission to feel and it was worth it. I am in control of my thoughts and my life. When other people hurt me I have the power to tell them how what they did made me feel. I have the power to decide what no longer serves me and I will release it with ease. I can do things that feel hard. Everything I need is available to me. I am in the process of healing. Today I learned more about who I want to be and what I want in my life. My purpose was created just for me. I will use my gifts and talents to serve now as I grow in my purpose. My heart is growing. I am grateful because I am learning what it means to love, honor, and see me.

CHAPTER 15

Day 5

(Fill in the blanks)

This morning I feel :

Today I will focus on :

I feel the most loved and like my life when I am doing :

Today I had to deal with :

What are my feelings on what I had to deal with today? What was the real issue? Did I carry any biases about myself or others?

Which one of my basic needs felt threatened?

How can I reframe what I dealt with today? What was it teaching me?

What kind of support do I need to move past this?

Do I need some time alone or do I need to practice the speaker/ listener technique with someone?

Nightly Mantra :

Today I did my best. Today I was enough. Today God was watching over me. I gave myself permission to feel and it was worth it. I am in control of my thoughts and my life. When other people hurt me I have the power to tell them how what they did made me feel. I have the power to decide what no longer serves me and I will release it with ease. I can do things that feel hard. Everything I need is available to me. I am in the process of healing. Today I learned more about who I want to be and what I want in my life. My purpose was created just for me. I will use my gifts and talents to serve now as I grow in my purpose. My heart is growing. I am grateful because I am learning what it means to love, honor, and see me.

CHAPTER 16

Day 6

(Fill in the blanks)

This morning I feel :

Today I will focus on :

I feel the most loved and like my life when I am doing :

Today I had to deal with :

What are my feelings on what I had to deal with today? What was the real issue? Did I carry any biases about myself or others?

Which one of my basic needs felt threatened?

How can I reframe what I dealt with today? What was it teaching me?

What kind of support do I need to move past this?

Do I need some time alone or do I need to practice the speaker/listener technique with someone?

Nightly Mantra :

Today I did my best. Today I was enough. Today God was watching over me. I gave myself permission to feel and it was worth it. I am in control of my thoughts and my life. When other people hurt me I have the power to tell them how what they did made me feel. I have the power to decide what no longer serves me and I will release it with ease. I can do things that feel hard. Everything I need is available to me. I am in the process of healing. Today I learned more about who I want to be and what I want in my life. My purpose was created just for me. I will use my gifts and talents to serve now as I grow in my purpose. My heart is growing. I am grateful because I am learning what it means to love, honor, and see me.

CHAPTER 17

Day 7

(Fill in the blanks)

This morning I feel :

Today I will focus on :

I feel the most loved and like my life when I am doing :

Today I had to deal with :

What are my feelings on what I had to deal with today? What was the real issue? Did I carry any biases about myself or others?

Which one of my basic needs felt threatened?

How can I reframe what I dealt with today? What was it teaching me?

What kind of support do I need to move past this?

Do I need some time alone or do I need to practice the speaker/
listener technique with someone?

Nightly Mantra :

Today I did my best. Today I was enough. Today God was watching over me. I gave myself permission to feel and it was worth it. I am in control of my thoughts and my life. When other people hurt me I have the power to tell them how what they did made me feel. I have the power to decide what no longer serves me and I will release it with ease. I can do things that feel hard. Everything I need is available to me. I am in the process of healing. Today I learned more about who I want to be and what I want in my life. My purpose was created just for me. I will use my gifts and talents to serve now as I grow in my purpose. My heart is growing. I am grateful because I am learning what it means to love, honor, and see me.

CHAPTER 18

Day 8

(Fill in the blanks)

This morning I feel :

Today I will focus on :

I feel the most loved and like my life when I am doing :

Today I had to deal with :

What are my feelings on what I had to deal with today? What was the real issue? Did I carry any biases about myself or others?

Which one of my basic needs felt threatened?

How can I reframe what I dealt with today? What was it teaching me?

What kind of support do I need to move past this?

Do I need some time alone or do I need to practice the speaker/
listener technique with someone?

Nightly Mantra :

Today I did my best. Today I was enough. Today God was watching over me. I gave myself permission to feel and it was worth it. I am in control of my thoughts and my life. When other people hurt me I have the power to tell them how what they did made me feel. I have the power to decide what no longer serves me and I will release it with ease. I can do things that feel hard. Everything I need is available to me. I am in the process of healing. Today I learned more about who I want to be and what I want in my life. My purpose was created just for me. I will use my gifts and talents to serve now as I grow in my purpose. My heart is growing. I am grateful because I am learning what it means to love, honor, and see me.

CHAPTER 19

Day 9

(Fill in the blanks)

This morning I feel :

Today I will focus on :

I feel the most loved and like my life when I am doing :

Today I had to deal with :

What are my feelings on what I had to deal with today? What was the real issue? Did I carry any biases about myself or others?

Which one of my basic needs felt threatened?

How can I reframe what I dealt with today? What was it teaching me?

What kind of support do I need to move past this?

Do I need some time alone or do I need to practice the speaker/listener technique with someone?

Nightly Mantra :

Today I did my best. Today I was enough. Today God was watching over me. I gave myself permission to feel and it was worth it. I am in control of my thoughts and my life. When other people hurt me I have the power to tell them how what they did made me feel. I have the power to decide what no longer serves me and I will release it with ease. I can do things that feel hard. Everything I need is available to me. I am in the process of healing. Today I learned more about who I want to be and what I want in my life. My purpose was created just for me. I will use my gifts and talents to serve now as I grow in my purpose. My heart is growing. I am grateful because I am learning what it means to love, honor, and see me.

CHAPTER 20

Day 10

(Fill in the blanks)

This morning I feel :

Today I will focus on :

I feel the most loved and like my life when I am doing :

Today I had to deal with :

What are my feelings on what I had to deal with today? What was the real issue? Did I carry any biases about myself or others?

Which one of my basic needs felt threatened?

How can I reframe what I dealt with today? What was it teaching me?

What kind of support do I need to move past this?

Do I need some time alone or do I need to practice the speaker/
listener technique with someone?

Nightly Mantra :

Today I did my best. Today I was enough. Today God was watching over me. I gave myself permission to feel and it was worth it. I am in control of my thoughts and my life. When other people hurt me I have the power to tell them how what they did made me feel. I have the power to decide what no longer serves me and I will release it with ease. I can do things that feel hard. Everything I need is available to me. I am in the process of healing. Today I learned more about who I want to be and what I want in my life. My purpose was created just for me. I will use my gifts and talents to serve now as I grow in my purpose. My heart is growing. I am grateful because I am learning what it means to love, honor, and see me.

CHAPTER 21

Day 11

(Fill in the blanks)

This morning I feel :

Today I will focus on :

I feel the most loved and like my life when I am doing :

Today I had to deal with :

What are my feelings on what I had to deal with today? What was the real issue? Did I carry any biases about myself or others?

Which one of my basic needs felt threatened?

How can I reframe what I dealt with today? What was it teaching me?

What kind of support do I need to move past this?

Do I need some time alone or do I need to practice the speaker/ listener technique with someone?

Nightly Mantra :

Today I did my best. Today I was enough. Today God was watching over me. I gave myself permission to feel and it was worth it. I am in control of my thoughts and my life. When other people hurt me I have the power to tell them how what they did made me feel. I have the power to decide what no longer serves me and I will release it with ease. I can do things that feel hard. Everything I need is available to me. I am in the process of healing. Today I learned more about who I want to be and what I want in my life. My purpose was created just for me. I will use my gifts and talents to serve now as I grow in my purpose. My heart is growing. I am grateful because I am learning what it means to love, honor, and see me.

CHAPTER 22

Day 12

(Fill in the blanks)

This morning I feel :

Today I will focus on :

I feel the most loved and like my life when I am doing :

Today I had to deal with :

What are my feelings on what I had to deal with today? What was the real issue? Did I carry any biases about myself or others?

Which one of my basic needs felt threatened?

How can I reframe what I dealt with today? What was it teaching me?

What kind of support do I need to move past this?

Do I need some time alone or do I need to practice the speaker/
listener technique with someone?

Nightly Mantra :

Today I did my best. Today I was enough. Today God was watching over me. I gave myself permission to feel and it was worth it. I am in control of my thoughts and my life. When other people hurt me I have the power to tell them how what they did made me feel. I have the power to decide what no longer serves me and I will release it with ease. I can do things that feel hard. Everything I need is available to me. I am in the process of healing. Today I learned more about who I want to be and what I want in my life. My purpose was created just for me. I will use my gifts and talents to serve now as I grow in my purpose. My heart is growing. I am grateful because I am learning what it means to love, honor, and see me.

CHAPTER 23

Day 13

(Fill in the blanks)

This morning I feel :

Today I will focus on :

I feel the most loved and like my life when I am doing :

Today I had to deal with :

What are my feelings on what I had to deal with today? What was the real issue? Did I carry any biases about myself or others?

Which one of my basic needs felt threatened?

How can I reframe what I dealt with today? What was it teaching me?

What kind of support do I need to move past this?

Do I need some time alone or do I need to practice the speaker/listener technique with someone?

Nightly Mantra :

Today I did my best. Today I was enough. Today God was watching over me. I gave myself permission to feel and it was worth it. I am in control of my thoughts and my life. When other people hurt me I have the power to tell them how what they did made me feel. I have the power to decide what no longer serves me and I will release it with ease. I can do things that feel hard. Everything I need is available to me. I am in the process of healing. Today I learned more about who I want to be and what I want in my life. My purpose was created just for me. I will use my gifts and talents to serve now as I grow in my purpose. My heart is growing. I am grateful because I am learning what it means to love, honor, and see me.

CHAPTER 24

Day 14

(Fill in the blanks)

This morning I feel :

Today I will focus on :

I feel the most loved and like my life when I am doing :

Today I had to deal with :

What are my feelings on what I had to deal with today? What was the real issue? Did I carry any biases about myself or others?

Which one of my basic needs felt threatened?

How can I reframe what I dealt with today? What was it teaching me?

What kind of support do I need to move past this?

Do I need some time alone or do I need to practice the speaker/
listener technique with someone?

Nightly Mantra :

Today I did my best. Today I was enough. Today God was watching over me. I gave myself permission to feel and it was worth it. I
am in control of my thoughts and my life. When other people hurt
me I have the power to tell them how what they did made me feel. I
have the power to decide what no longer serves me and I will release
it with ease. I can do things that feel hard. Everything I need is
available to me. I am in the process of healing. Today I learned more
about who I want to be and what I want in my life. My purpose was
created just for me. I will use my gifts and talents to serve now as I
grow in my purpose. My heart is growing. I am grateful because I
am learning what it means to love, honor, and see me.

Day 15

(Fill in the blanks)

This morning I feel :

Today I will focus on :

I feel the most loved and like my life when I am doing :

Today I had to deal with :

What are my feelings on what I had to deal with today? What was the real issue? Did I carry any biases about myself or others?

Which one of my basic needs felt threatened?

How can I reframe what I dealt with today? What was it teaching me?

What kind of support do I need to move past this?

Do I need some time alone or do I need to practice the speaker/
listener technique with someone?

Nightly Mantra :

Today I did my best. Today I was enough. Today God was watching over me. I gave myself permission to feel and it was worth it. I am in control of my thoughts and my life. When other people hurt me I have the power to tell them how what they did made me feel. I have the power to decide what no longer serves me and I will release it with ease. I can do things that feel hard. Everything I need is available to me. I am in the process of healing. Today I learned more about who I want to be and what I want in my life. My purpose was created just for me. I will use my gifts and talents to serve now as I grow in my purpose. My heart is growing. I am grateful because I am learning what it means to love, honor, and see me.

CHAPTER 26

Day 16

(Fill in the blanks)

This morning I feel :

Today I will focus on :

I feel the most loved and like my life when I am doing :

Today I had to deal with :

What are my feelings on what I had to deal with today? What was the real issue? Did I carry any biases about myself or others?

Which one of my basic needs felt threatened?

How can I reframe what I dealt with today? What was it teaching me?

What kind of support do I need to move past this?

Do I need some time alone or do I need to practice the speaker/listener technique with someone?

Nightly Mantra :

Today I did my best. Today I was enough. Today God was watching over me. I gave myself permission to feel and it was worth it. I am in control of my thoughts and my life. When other people hurt me I have the power to tell them how what they did made me feel. I have the power to decide what no longer serves me and I will release it with ease. I can do things that feel hard. Everything I need is available to me. I am in the process of healing. Today I learned more about who I want to be and what I want in my life. My purpose was created just for me. I will use my gifts and talents to serve now as I grow in my purpose. My heart is growing. I am grateful because I am learning what it means to love, honor, and see me.

CHAPTER 27

Day 17

(Fill in the blanks)

This morning I feel :

Today I will focus on :

I feel the most loved and like my life when I am doing :

Today I had to deal with :

What are my feelings on what I had to deal with today? What was the real issue? Did I carry any biases about myself or others?

Which one of my basic needs felt threatened?

How can I reframe what I dealt with today? What was it teaching me?

What kind of support do I need to move past this?

Do I need some time alone or do I need to practice the speaker/listener technique with someone?

Nightly Mantra :

Today I did my best. Today I was enough. Today God was watching over me. I gave myself permission to feel and it was worth it. I am in control of my thoughts and my life. When other people hurt me I have the power to tell them how what they did made me feel. I have the power to decide what no longer serves me and I will release it with ease. I can do things that feel hard. Everything I need is available to me. I am in the process of healing. Today I learned more about who I want to be and what I want in my life. My purpose was created just for me. I will use my gifts and talents to serve now as I grow in my purpose. My heart is growing. I am grateful because I am learning what it means to love, honor, and see me.

CHAPTER 28

Day 18

(Fill in the blanks)

This morning I feel :

Today I will focus on :

I feel the most loved and like my life when I am doing :

Today I had to deal with :

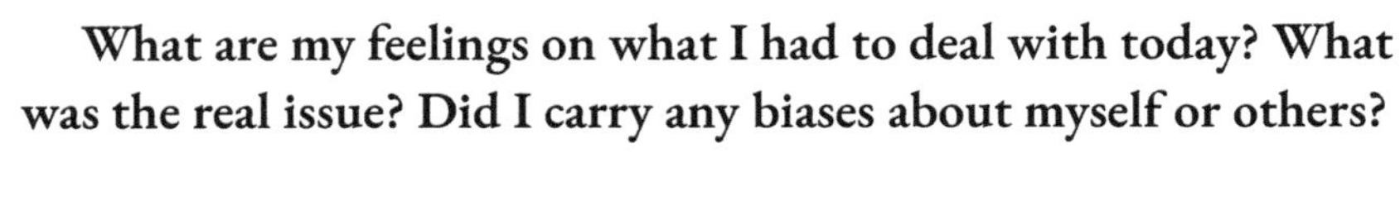

What are my feelings on what I had to deal with today? What was the real issue? Did I carry any biases about myself or others?

Which one of my basic needs felt threatened?

How can I reframe what I dealt with today? What was it teaching me?

What kind of support do I need to move past this?

Do I need some time alone or do I need to practice the speaker/listener technique with someone?

Nightly Mantra :

Today I did my best. Today I was enough. Today God was watching over me. I gave myself permission to feel and it was worth it. I am in control of my thoughts and my life. When other people hurt me I have the power to tell them how what they did made me feel. I have the power to decide what no longer serves me and I will release it with ease. I can do things that feel hard. Everything I need is available to me. I am in the process of healing. Today I learned more about who I want to be and what I want in my life. My purpose was created just for me. I will use my gifts and talents to serve now as I grow in my purpose. My heart is growing. I am grateful because I am learning what it means to love, honor, and see me.

Day 19

(Fill in the blanks)

This morning I feel :

Today I will focus on :

I feel the most loved and like my life when I am doing :

Today I had to deal with :

What are my feelings on what I had to deal with today? What was the real issue? Did I carry any biases about myself or others?

Which one of my basic needs felt threatened?

How can I reframe what I dealt with today? What was it teaching me?

What kind of support do I need to move past this?

Do I need some time alone or do I need to practice the speaker/listener technique with someone?

Nightly Mantra :

Today I did my best. Today I was enough. Today God was watching over me. I gave myself permission to feel and it was worth it. I am in control of my thoughts and my life. When other people hurt me I have the power to tell them how what they did made me feel. I have the power to decide what no longer serves me and I will release it with ease. I can do things that feel hard. Everything I need is available to me. I am in the process of healing. Today I learned more about who I want to be and what I want in my life. My purpose was created just for me. I will use my gifts and talents to serve now as I grow in my purpose. My heart is growing. I am grateful because I am learning what it means to love, honor, and see me.

CHAPTER 30

Day 20

(Fill in the blanks)

This morning I feel :

Today I will focus on :

I feel the most loved and like my life when I am doing :

Today I had to deal with :

What are my feelings on what I had to deal with today? What was the real issue? Did I carry any biases about myself or others?

Which one of my basic needs felt threatened?

How can I reframe what I dealt with today? What was it teaching me?

What kind of support do I need to move past this?

Do I need some time alone or do I need to practice the speaker/
listener technique with someone?

Nightly Mantra :

Today I did my best. Today I was enough. Today God was watching over me. I gave myself permission to feel and it was worth it. I am in control of my thoughts and my life. When other people hurt me I have the power to tell them how what they did made me feel. I have the power to decide what no longer serves me and I will release it with ease. I can do things that feel hard. Everything I need is available to me. I am in the process of healing. Today I learned more about who I want to be and what I want in my life. My purpose was created just for me. I will use my gifts and talents to serve now as I grow in my purpose. My heart is growing. I am grateful because I am learning what it means to love, honor, and see me.

Day 21

(Fill in the blanks)

This morning I feel :

Today I will focus on :

I feel the most loved and like my life when I am doing :

Today I had to deal with :

What are my feelings on what I had to deal with today? What was the real issue? Did I carry any biases about myself or others?

Which one of my basic needs felt threatened?

How can I reframe what I dealt with today? What was it teaching me?

What kind of support do I need to move past this?

Do I need some time alone or do I need to practice the speaker/listener technique with someone?

Nightly Mantra :

Today I did my best. Today I was enough. Today God was watching over me. I gave myself permission to feel and it was worth it. I am in control of my thoughts and my life. When other people hurt me I have the power to tell them how what they did made me feel. I have the power to decide what no longer serves me and I will release it with ease. I can do things that feel hard. Everything I need is available to me. I am in the process of healing. Today I learned more about who I want to be and what I want in my life. My purpose was created just for me. I will use my gifts and talents to serve now as I grow in my purpose. My heart is growing. I am grateful because I am learning what it means to love, honor, and see me.

CHAPTER 32

Day 22

(Fill in the blanks)

This morning I feel :

Today I will focus on :

I feel the most loved and like my life when I am doing :

Today I had to deal with :

What are my feelings on what I had to deal with today? What was the real issue? Did I carry any biases about myself or others?

Which one of my basic needs felt threatened?

How can I reframe what I dealt with today? What was it teaching me?

What kind of support do I need to move past this?

Do I need some time alone or do I need to practice the speaker/
listener technique with someone?

Nightly Mantra :

Today I did my best. Today I was enough. Today God was watching over me. I gave myself permission to feel and it was worth it. I
am in control of my thoughts and my life. When other people hurt
me I have the power to tell them how what they did made me feel. I
have the power to decide what no longer serves me and I will release
it with ease. I can do things that feel hard. Everything I need is
available to me. I am in the process of healing. Today I learned more
about who I want to be and what I want in my life. My purpose was
created just for me. I will use my gifts and talents to serve now as I
grow in my purpose. My heart is growing. I am grateful because I
am learning what it means to love, honor, and see me.

Day 23

(Fill in the blanks)

This morning I feel :

Today I will focus on :

I feel the most loved and like my life when I am doing :

Today I had to deal with :

What are my feelings on what I had to deal with today? What was the real issue? Did I carry any biases about myself or others?

Which one of my basic needs felt threatened?

How can I reframe what I dealt with today? What was it teaching me?

What kind of support do I need to move past this?

Do I need some time alone or do I need to practice the speaker/listener technique with someone?

Nightly Mantra :

Today I did my best. Today I was enough. Today God was watching over me. I gave myself permission to feel and it was worth it. I am in control of my thoughts and my life. When other people hurt me I have the power to tell them how what they did made me feel. I have the power to decide what no longer serves me and I will release it with ease. I can do things that feel hard. Everything I need is available to me. I am in the process of healing. Today I learned more about who I want to be and what I want in my life. My purpose was created just for me. I will use my gifts and talents to serve now as I grow in my purpose. My heart is growing. I am grateful because I am learning what it means to love, honor, and see me.

CHAPTER 34

Day 24

(Fill in the blanks)

This morning I feel :

Today I will focus on :

I feel the most loved and like my life when I am doing :

Today I had to deal with :

What are my feelings on what I had to deal with today? What was the real issue? Did I carry any biases about myself or others?

Which one of my basic needs felt threatened?

How can I reframe what I dealt with today? What was it teaching me?

What kind of support do I need to move past this?

Do I need some time alone or do I need to practice the speaker/
listener technique with someone?

Nightly Mantra :

Today I did my best. Today I was enough. Today God was watching over me. I gave myself permission to feel and it was worth it. I am in control of my thoughts and my life. When other people hurt me I have the power to tell them how what they did made me feel. I have the power to decide what no longer serves me and I will release it with ease. I can do things that feel hard. Everything I need is available to me. I am in the process of healing. Today I learned more about who I want to be and what I want in my life. My purpose was created just for me. I will use my gifts and talents to serve now as I grow in my purpose. My heart is growing. I am grateful because I am learning what it means to love, honor, and see me.

CHAPTER 35

Day 25

(Fill in the blanks)

This morning I feel :

Today I will focus on :

I feel the most loved and like my life when I am doing :

Today I had to deal with :

What are my feelings on what I had to deal with today? What was the real issue? Did I carry any biases about myself or others?

Which one of my basic needs felt threatened?

How can I reframe what I dealt with today? What was it teaching me?

What kind of support do I need to move past this?

Do I need some time alone or do I need to practice the speaker/listener technique with someone?

Nightly Mantra :

Today I did my best. Today I was enough. Today God was watching over me. I gave myself permission to feel and it was worth it. I am in control of my thoughts and my life. When other people hurt me I have the power to tell them how what they did made me feel. I have the power to decide what no longer serves me and I will release it with ease. I can do things that feel hard. Everything I need is available to me. I am in the process of healing. Today I learned more about who I want to be and what I want in my life. My purpose was created just for me. I will use my gifts and talents to serve now as I grow in my purpose. My heart is growing. I am grateful because I am learning what it means to love, honor, and see me.

CHAPTER 36

Day 26

(Fill in the blanks)

This morning I feel :

Today I will focus on :

I feel the most loved and like my life when I am doing :

Today I had to deal with :

What are my feelings on what I had to deal with today? What was the real issue? Did I carry any biases about myself or others?

Which one of my basic needs felt threatened?

How can I reframe what I dealt with today? What was it teaching me?

What kind of support do I need to move past this?

Do I need some time alone or do I need to practice the speaker/listener technique with someone?

Nightly Mantra :

Today I did my best. Today I was enough. Today God was watching over me. I gave myself permission to feel and it was worth it. I am in control of my thoughts and my life. When other people hurt me I have the power to tell them how what they did made me feel. I have the power to decide what no longer serves me and I will release it with ease. I can do things that feel hard. Everything I need is available to me. I am in the process of healing. Today I learned more about who I want to be and what I want in my life. My purpose was created just for me. I will use my gifts and talents to serve now as I grow in my purpose. My heart is growing. I am grateful because I am learning what it means to love, honor, and see me.

CHAPTER 37

Day 27

(Fill in the blanks)

This morning I feel :

Today I will focus on :

I feel the most loved and like my life when I am doing :

Today I had to deal with :

What are my feelings on what I had to deal with today? What was the real issue? Did I carry any biases about myself or others?

Which one of my basic needs felt threatened?

How can I reframe what I dealt with today? What was it teaching me?

What kind of support do I need to move past this?

Do I need some time alone or do I need to practice the speaker/listener technique with someone?

Nightly Mantra :

Today I did my best. Today I was enough. Today God was watching over me. I gave myself permission to feel and it was worth it. I am in control of my thoughts and my life. When other people hurt me I have the power to tell them how what they did made me feel. I have the power to decide what no longer serves me and I will release it with ease. I can do things that feel hard. Everything I need is available to me. I am in the process of healing. Today I learned more about who I want to be and what I want in my life. My purpose was created just for me. I will use my gifts and talents to serve now as I grow in my purpose. My heart is growing. I am grateful because I am learning what it means to love, honor, and see me.

CHAPTER 38

Day 28

(Fill in the blanks)

This morning I feel :

Today I will focus on :

I feel the most loved and like my life when I am doing :

Today I had to deal with :

What are my feelings on what I had to deal with today? What was the real issue? Did I carry any biases about myself or others?

Which one of my basic needs felt threatened?

How can I reframe what I dealt with today? What was it teaching me?

What kind of support do I need to move past this?

Do I need some time alone or do I need to practice the speaker/listener technique with someone?

Nightly Mantra :

Today I did my best. Today I was enough. Today God was watching over me. I gave myself permission to feel and it was worth it. I am in control of my thoughts and my life. When other people hurt me I have the power to tell them how what they did made me feel. I have the power to decide what no longer serves me and I will release it with ease. I can do things that feel hard. Everything I need is available to me. I am in the process of healing. Today I learned more about who I want to be and what I want in my life. My purpose was created just for me. I will use my gifts and talents to serve now as I grow in my purpose. My heart is growing. I am grateful because I am learning what it means to love, honor, and see me.

CHAPTER 39

Day 29

(Fill in the blanks)

This morning I feel :

Today I will focus on :

I feel the most loved and like my life when I am doing :

Today I had to deal with :

What are my feelings on what I had to deal with today? What was the real issue? Did I carry any biases about myself or others?

Which one of my basic needs felt threatened?

How can I reframe what I dealt with today? What was it teaching me?

What kind of support do I need to move past this?

Do I need some time alone or do I need to practice the speaker/listener technique with someone?

Nightly Mantra :

Today I did my best. Today I was enough. Today God was watching over me. I gave myself permission to feel and it was worth it. I am in control of my thoughts and my life. When other people hurt me I have the power to tell them how what they did made me feel. I have the power to decide what no longer serves me and I will release it with ease. I can do things that feel hard. Everything I need is available to me. I am in the process of healing. Today I learned more about who I want to be and what I want in my life. My purpose was created just for me. I will use my gifts and talents to serve now as I grow in my purpose. My heart is growing. I am grateful because I am learning what it means to love, honor, and see me.

CHAPTER 40

Day 30

(Fill in the blanks)

This morning I feel :

Today I will focus on :

I feel the most loved and like my life when I am doing :

Today I had to deal with :

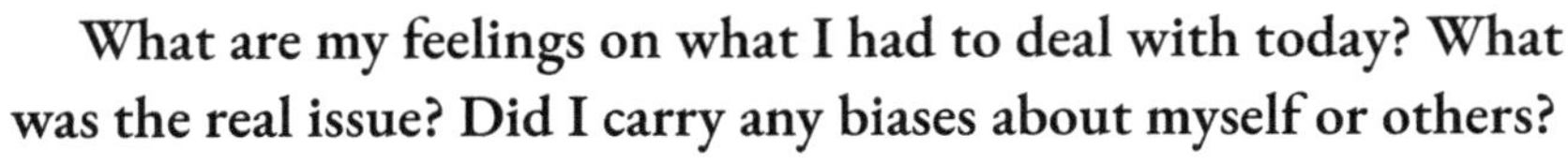

What are my feelings on what I had to deal with today? What was the real issue? Did I carry any biases about myself or others?

Which one of my basic needs felt threatened?

How can I reframe what I dealt with today? What was it teaching me?

What kind of support do I need to move past this?

Do I need some time alone or do I need to practice the speaker/
listener technique with someone?

Nightly Mantra :

Today I did my best. Today I was enough. Today God was watching over me. I gave myself permission to feel and it was worth it. I am in control of my thoughts and my life. When other people hurt me I have the power to tell them how what they did made me feel. I have the power to decide what no longer serves me and I will release it with ease. I can do things that feel hard. Everything I need is available to me. I am in the process of healing. Today I learned more about who I want to be and what I want in my life. My purpose was created just for me. I will use my gifts and talents to serve now as I grow in my purpose. My heart is growing. I am grateful because I am learning what it means to love, honor, and see me.

Shari Green is the coach you wish you met sooner. She is a faith-filled wife, mother, author, Certified N.L.P. Practitioner and Mindset Coach that believes everyday women should have the tools to guide themselves towards mental fitness. For so many years, she struggled with seeing herself as unworthy and dealing with so much anger. After losing two children, she discovered that every pain in her life had built her endurance and faith to take on more significant challenges and see greater value in her life. Her bold faith and mindset management caused her to push past every traumatic experience in her life and place her on her true path of purpose, helping women like you overcome everything that stands in your way of personal fulfillment and purpose.

Get access to **FREE Mindset Training** and receive weekly tips by emailing **contact@sharigreencoaching.com.**
Place "Heal" in the subject title.

Get To See Behind The Scenes Of My World on Instagram
@sharigreencoaching